"Just Hangin' Out, Ma"

Anecdotes and Tales From the Old Neighborhood

Lawrence - My Hometown

"Just Hangin' Out, Ma"

Anecdotes and Tales From the Old Neighborhood

Lawrence - My Hometown
Richard Edward Noble

Published in the United States of America
By
Noble Publishing
889 C.C. Land Road
Eastpoint, Florida 32328
www.richardedwardnoble@fairpoint.net

Interior layout and design by
Carol Noble

4

Dedicated To

Christine Lewis

Thank you Christine, your interest and enthusiasm stimulated a new adventure of writing fun and enjoyment for me. You have been inspirational. Without your efforts, I doubt this book would ever have been created.

Introduction

Lawrence – My Hometown

Thank God for the street corners of Lawrence, Massachusetts and being able to hang out.

I started writing stories about the old gang and hangin' out when I was about eighteen years old. Then life came along and got in my way. But now I'm back. And as far as I am concerned, I'm stronger and better equipped to do justice to the old gang and the street corners that made our hangin' out so memorable.

This is my first book on this subject and it covers more than just the variety stores, drugstores and street corners of my youth. It branches out into barrooms, nightclubs, poolrooms, bowling alleys and the complete Full Monty of the "I'm just hangin' out, Ma" experience.

I hope you all enjoy this adventure, feel the love, get the jokes and have some laughs.

The movie *The Full Monty* reminded me of my hometown of Lawrence. An old industrial mill town filled with blue collar workers, "regular" type people and semi-abandoned, mile long, redbrick, textile mills everywhere.

I would like to say we were middle class but after the mills left town for greener pastures and cheaper labor and the unemployment proliferated, we were poor. We thought of ourselves as middle class though. If we weren't, we sure wanted to be.

I never thought of my town as a ghetto. That would be too radical. We were tenement dwellers for the most part and strongly Roman Catholic. That translated into lots and lots of kids "hangin' out" at every corner variety store and any available street corner, driving the neighbors nuts and keeping the cops busy.

7

We were ethnic. Lawrence to this day calls itself "the Immigrant City." We claimed over 40 different nationalities, mostly eastern and western European. All of us had grandparents who garbled some kind of foreign mumbo-jumbo or chanted with an accent so thick none of us kids knew what the heck they were talking about. Our generation had been Americanized even if our parents or grandparents were still fantasizing about "the Old World."

Times were tough in the 40's, 50's and 60's when I was growing up. The streets and the "gang" were our refuge from the constant bickering back home in the apartment. The gang was a part of my family. My fondest memories of growing up are of my street corner buddies.

"Where you goin', son?"

"Up the corner, Ma."

"And what ya gonna do up the corner, son?"

"We're just hangin' out, Ma. That's all, just hangin' out."

Contents

Bea's Sandwich Shop

Bea's sandwich shop was a big memory for those of us who were growing up in the 50's and 60's in good old Lawrence, Massachusetts.

There was a whole legend that went along with the success of Bea's sandwich shop. My older brother told me that the fable was true. Richie Consoli and his younger brother Bobby were running the shop when we were kids.

Supposedly, their parents, the founders of the shop began their operation in their tenement kitchen. They would prepare their famous cutlet sandwich and then sell it from a mobile cart they pushed down onto Broadway — so claimed the legend.

They started out selling their sandwiches at lunch time to the kids from Central Catholic and Lawrence High. In time, they rented or bought a building on Broadway and opened their first shop.

The shop itself was rather revolutionary. It had no places to sit. The walls were covered with mirrors. A counter ran below the mirrors on both walls. The entrance and building front were large glass windows. One could drive by on Broadway and see if they were busy or not. McDonald's and Burger King and most of the fast food shops adopted that idea. But Bea's came before any McDonald's and certainly before any McDonald's came to the Lawrence area.

The kitchen was also quite revolutionary. The ordering area was glass and the entire kitchen could be observed by the customers. If anybody dropped a cutlet on the floor it had to go into the garbage or everyone would know. The employees had to look clean and presentable also. And they did. A few daubs of spaghetti sauce on the apron did not warrant any comment or customer disapproval. This "open kitchen" idea was big in the restaurant business in the 70's. I was a cook in one such open kitchen. It wasn't pretty.

Eventually, Bea's had a whole wall menu full of cutlet sandwich varieties and several outlets – cutlet with plain sauce, cutlet with meat sauce, cutlet with meat sauce and mushrooms, cutlet with green peppers and onions and on and on. But once they had their shop opened, they presented other sandwich favorites. Their Chicken bar-b-que was a big one. I think they called it Chicken a la king which was more appropriate. The sandwich had nothing to do with bar-b-que sauce or smoked meat. It was chicken with a mayonnaise or cream sauce of some kind. It was great.

They also had hot dogs. They were boiled in beer, I was told. Of course they had sausage and meatball sandwiches and several other Italian favorites. Eventually they built a state-of-the-art shop out on route 110, then another in Haverhill, one in Lowell and another at Hampton Beach. We all thought that Bea's was going to become a national chain or franchise, but something went awry. Today they have all disappeared.

When I was a little guy my uncle used to take me down to Bea's. I always ordered a cutlet. He ordered the Chicken-a-la-king. The cutlet was only thirty-five cents and it was too big to fit in the sub bun. You would have to eat the cutlet down around the edges before you got to the bun. In my childhood memories it was a giant sandwich. There was nothing else like it. My uncle's chicken

12

sandwich was also thirty-five cents, as I remember. It was the size of a regular, dinky hamburger. I often questioned my uncle's judgment on that account.

There was another fellow down the street, King-size Sandwich Shop, who always bragged that he used real veal in his veal cutlets and not cheap pork butt like they used at Bea's. He would point up to his sign and make note that he used the word "veal" while Bea's only used the word "cutlet." His cutlet was good too. But it didn't flop out over the edge of the bun by three inches like Bea's. It was certainly "softer" (more tender) than Bea's. But, it was no contest. Everybody liked the Bea's pounded pork butt cutlet better than anybody else's.

When we were early teenagers we would head down to Bea's and buy sauce sandwiches. They were ten cents. They weren't on the menu but all us kids knew about them. They would slop a big ladle of their homemade meat sauce into one of their delicious buns. Sometimes we would get two or three sauce sandwiches each.

One day a mob of us walked down there. We pooled all our money. We had enough money to buy 37 sauce sandwiches. It was a little embarrassing to be ordering sauce sandwiches, so we drew straws to see who would get the honor of going inside and ordering 37 sauce sandwiches.

Jack Sheehy, who grew up to own the Pizza Pub on Lawrence St., got the honor. Jack was a little shy in those days. So when he went up to the window he whispered to the girl taking his order: "Thirty-seven sauce sandwiches, please."

When they called his number and he went to the window, the girl said, "That will be fifty-four dollars," or some such phenomenal amount. Jack protested quietly but vigorously. "It can't be. It is only supposed to be $3.70 for 37 sauce sandwiches."

The girl said, "You ordered sausage sandwiches."

"God no," Jack squealed. "I ordered sauce sandwiches. I only have $3.70."

The girl frowned and then brought all the sandwiches back to the cook. He had a very bad look on his face as he pealed all the sausages out of our 37 sauce sandwiches.

When the girl returned with the sauce sandwiches she didn't call out our number. She used the loud speaker and said, "Would the young man who ordered 37 sauce sandwiches please come to the pickup window." As I remember, Jack attempted to walk out the front door but we would not let him do it. We wanted our sauce sandwiches even at the price of Jack's humiliation.

We have been laughing over that story now for 50 years. Every time someone tells it, it gets more hilarious. Amazingly enough I can remember that incident as if it were yesterday but remembering what actually happened yesterday is an entirely different story.

Little Criminals

I was reading a book not too long ago by the infamous bank robber, Willie Sutton. Besides robbing banks and breaking out of prisons all over America, Willie had a famous quote attached to his legend. When asked why he robbed banks, his alleged response was, "Because that's where the money is."

As I continued reading his autobiography, I noticed that Willie and I had a number of similar attitudes and opinions. Willie did not "rat" on his fellow riffraff. He didn't like wealthy people very much. He justified his robbing banks by suggesting that it was only fair because, in his opinion, banks robbed regular people and on a regular basis. He was also not overly fond of policemen, politicians, or authority in general.

As I continued reading Willie Sutton, I wondered why an upstanding, righteous, asset to the community like me was so sympathetic to the views of a professional bank robber.

One of the first books from the Lawrence Public Library that I read as a young man was the Great Impostor, written about the phenomenal life of Ferdinand Waldo Demara. The author was Robert Crichton. I picked the book because Mr. Demara was from Lawrence.

Ferdinand Waldo Demara got drafted but went AWOL. He then falsified documents, turned himself into a

Harvard professor and got a commission in the Marine Corps. He continued on a road of imaginative deception and assumed a number of other difficult and prestigious occupations.

They made a movie about him staring Tony Curtis, Karl Malden, Raymond Massey and an array of other big movie stars.

So why am I reading about criminals and enjoying it? Why do I have so many common criminal values? Could it have anything to do with being raised in poverty in the streets of Lawrence and being chased around every day, from corner to corner, by the local "flatfoots"?

Well whatever the sociological and psychological connections, us little guys hangin' out on the street corners of Lawrence in the 50's and 60's did not have the healthiest attitude towards the local police. We weren't criminals or impostors. We lived there. But wherever it was that we decided to hang out, the police would soon be there to protest our right to squat.

In the early days of our street corner lives whenever the cops would pull up we would immediately scatter. But as time went on we became immune. They would take out their pencils and pads and ask us our names. We would lie. They would ask us where we lived and we would lie.

One day this cop decides he has taken all the guff he is going to, he says; "If you guys don't start answering me truthfully, you are all going to the station house."

His next question was, "Are you the oldest in your family?"

Ray Dolan said, "No, my mother and father are both older."

"That's it," the frustrated cop said. "Every one of you guys is under arrest and you are going with me down to the police station."

"No foolin'?" says Billy Jackson.

"No! I ain't foolin! Get over there and get into that cruiser."

Jackson jumped off the steps at Nell's Variety and ran towards the cruiser screaming, "Shot-gun. I got shot-gun. I yelled it first."

He ran over to the cruiser and jumped into the front passenger seat. When the cop climbed into the driver's seat, Jackson said, "Are you going to turn on the bubble machine and blast the siren?"

"Get the hell in the backseat, before I give you a crack."

"Oh, come on, man? How can six of us crowd into that tiny backseat?"

"MOVE!"

Jackson reluctantly climbed into the backseat with the rest of us. We bugged the cop all the way to the police station to turn on the siren and the bubble machine but he wouldn't do it.

They threw us into a room by ourselves. As I remember we pinched one pack of cigarettes and two brown bag lunches out of the desk in the room.

This guy came strolling in dressed in baggy pants and a holey T-shirt. He looked like he hadn't shaved in a week and slept in a garbage can the night before. Jack Greco said, "There's the Chief, now. Let's ask him about all this bull." We all laughed. Just then another officer stepped into the room, "Hey Chief, they need you downstairs."

"Tell them I'll be there in a minute," the bum replied.

That hobo was the chief!

Rambo had picked us up at about six p.m. By nine it started snowing heavy. We sat there until eleven or twelve o'clock. Finally the cop who arrested us came back into the room.

"What is it with you guys? Don't any of you have any parents?"

"Sure we got parents. Everybody's got parents."

"Well, it's midnight, and not one parent has called to find out where any of you juvenile delinquents are."

"Did you ever figure that our parents might not have telephones? And where do you get off calling us delinquents?"

"Well then, why haven't they showed up here at the station?"

"Why the heck would they look for us at the police station? They're probably wandering around the corner where you picked us up."

"Get the hell out of here and go home. I'm tired of looking at you guys."

"Screw you. You have to take us back to where you got us. It's been snowing for three hours. We'll freeze," said Jack Sheehy.

Believe it or not, the officer drove us back to the corner at Nell's and dumped us off. And all the way back we ragged him about the siren and the bubble machine. He turned them both on as he drove away. What a bugger!

Going to the RATS

RATS is STAR spelled backwards. The Star was a movie theater in North Lawrence. It was on the corner of Broadway and Daisy. I think Spruce St. became Daisy St. at some point but don't hold me to that. It has been a long time away from home for me.

We called the STAR the RATS because the Spicket River snaked behind the theater and the word around the playgrounds was that the STAR was infested with giant river rats.

I never saw any rats at the STAR. I remember the cats taking up position in front of the movie projector though. This precipitated the thunder of hundreds of tiny Buster Brown shoes or All Star Canvass sneakers pounding in unison on the theater floor. This thunder occurred when anything went awry in the projection room.

We often had to go wake the owner up. He and his wife collected and sold the tickets, popped the popcorn, staffed the candy counter, ran the projector and who knows what else.

Kids would bring rubber balls and "tonic" (soda pop) bottles to roll down the slope under the seats. When the object would hit somebody's shoe, there would be a scream, "A rat! A rat!" This was great fun for some; not so much for others.

The floor was so caked with sticky spilled soda and greasy popcorn butter (real butter), that when you walked between the rows your sneakers would stick to the floor. There was enough bubble gum under each seat to supply the entire continent of Asia. The seats were so old and worn that for many it was necessary to hang onto the arms of the chairs or else slide to the floor. Most kids solved that problem by putting their knees or their feet up against the back of the chair in front of them.

But with all its shortcomings, it was packed every Saturday afternoon for a kids' matinee. It was 12 cents to get in, but if you were able to scrounge up a quarter somewhere, you could get the special – admission plus popcorn and a soda or candy bar.

We saw some classic movies at the Star – *The Thing, The Blob, The Creature from the Black Lagoon, The Day the Earth Stood Still*, and of course, *Frankenstein.* I remember ducking under my seat at some of the scary parts. I was the kind of little kid who rode "the bench" on the merry-go-round at Salisbury Beach. It took me a year or two to graduate to a wooded horse that didn't go up and down. By the time that I was no longer afraid of the wooded horses that went up and down, I was too old to ride the merry-go-round anymore.

The afternoon matinee lasted all afternoon. The moms and dads loved it – and the kids did too. It seemed like they would show a hundred cartoons. We would see Bugs Bunny, Beep Beep the Road Runner, Porky Pig, Yosemite Sam and a million others. That would be followed by a serial. The serials were old silent movies. Simon Legree was big. He was mean. And the fair maiden was forever tied to a railroad track or hanging by a limb from a mountain top. Then we would see a newsreel – Edward R. Morrow or somebody like that.

We would see two full length features often interrupted by a sing-along where we would all "follow the bouncing ball." The words to a famous song would appear on the screen and the animated "bouncing ball" would hop along on top of the words striking out the notes. Believe it or not the kids liked that. But if you didn't, you could always take a trip to the snack bar and put a dime into the automatic tonic machine. You had to watch what you were doing at that soda machine. A paper cup would drop down onto a tray where it was supposed to be filled with syrup and carbonated water. But the darn cup would invariably drop into position with the bottom side up. If you weren't quick witted, your orange crush soda or RC cola would go right down the drain. And the owner would not give you another dime. That was learning personal responsibility the hard way!

But one of the biggest attractions of the Star Theater was to meet a boy or girl and hold hands – or whatever. No boy ever asked a girl to go to the Star with him. He would suggest a clandestine meeting. Sometimes the girls would even make the suggestion. Occasionally there would be an impromptu meeting precipitated by the question; Is this seat taken? Or, Can I sit with you?

One of my buddies had an impromptu meeting with just such a young lady. In the excitement of squeezing her elbow or shoulder, she was able to pick his back pocket and steal his wallet. He thought she was squeezing his butt. He felt that it was only fair to grant her the right to squeeze his butt in exchange for all of his illicit squeezing of her various body parts. He was very philosophic about the whole experience. He said his lost wallet would be forgotten one day but the memory of little Lulu's soft and tender "elbow" would last forever. This has proven to be correct.

There would be an usher walking around with a flashlight. He would shine his light and try to catch a couple embracing or as it was called "making out." If he did, he would admonish them. If the couple persisted or got caught several times the usher could ask them to leave the theater. I don't ever remember anyone getting bounced from the RATS for making out.

I always wondered if it was the usher and his persistent flashlight that generated the birthday parlor game called "Spotlight."

Spotlight was played at home at parties. The boys and girls would be randomly paired, the lights would be turned off, and the odd-man-out would try to catch a couple kissing with his flashlight so that he could change places with the boy caught in the light.

My god! Where were the parents in those days? I can hardly believe what I'm writing!

Black Horse Ale

My wife and I were back in Fort Lauderdale one Christmas for a break from our *Hobo-ing America* adventure of working our way around the U.S.A. Our homemade camper now sported an elevated fiberglass top (roof) we had installed while traveling through Riverside, California. We picked up my brother and his wife at their condo and took them for a hobo-style lunch on Fort Lauderdale beach.

We parked in one of the big, fancy hotel parking lots where we had a nice view of the beach. We opened the back doors to the van and sat at our makeshift dinner table drinking a beer and eating our sandwiches. As we sat there enjoying the view and the cool ocean breezes a party of six came out of the hotel's lounge. They were all dressed to the nines.

They were very happy as they came strolling by the open back doors of our van camper.

"Here, enjoy a real brew with your lunch," one of the entourage said hefting a six-pack of beer up onto our table.

"Why thank-you," I said sliding a bottle out of the six-pack and taking a look at the label. "This is a good brew," I said with emphasis. "I've downed a many of them in my day."

"That's impossible," the man said.

23

"Impossible my butt! I used to drink Holihan's Black Horse Ale all the time. It was manufactured and brewed right in my hometown. It is made with genuine spring water, you know."

"That's right," the man said. "Where's your hometown?"

"Lawrence, Massachusetts," I boasted.

"That's right again. But this company has been out of business for over a decade."

"Well, I'm not exactly a teenager," I said. "I've been drinking beer for a long time. In fact, I consider myself somewhat of a professional. This Holihan's Black Hose Ale is one of the best ales ever brewed," I flattered.

The man seemed to be beside himself with joy. He called his entire party over to the back of our camper. He introduced us to all his friends and then added, "We were impressed with this Holihan's Black Horse Ale ourselves. In fact, we just closed a deal inside that hotel. We bought the formula and the rights to this ale and we are going to start manufacturing it and distributing it all over America."

"No kidding! Well good luck to all of you."

"You guys must be a sign. What are the chances of meeting a group of people from Lawrence, Mass. in a parking lot at Fort Lauderdale beach after just signing a contract to buy the formula for Holihan's Black Horse Ale?"

"What are the odds on that?" I asked my brother Ernie who fancied himself to be a dog track handicapping expert. My brother moved to Florida because he had outgrown Rockingham Park in New Hampshire.

"I don't think you could get Nick the Greek to give you odds on that one."

The new Black Horse Ale owners went off laughing, hugging and slapping one another on the back.

My brother and I then went into reminiscing about Lawrence. We stopped when the girls began to doze off.

The Holihan brothers started their brewery in Lawrence in 1856, I discovered. In 1912, the name was changed to Diamond Spring Brewery and it was on Beacon Street. They were closed for the prohibition years but reopened in 1933. The Diamond Spring Brewery finally closed its doors in 1970.

The Peppermint Lounge

I was sitting at our cottage on Old Towne Way when Tommy Kabildis came rushing, breathless, through the door. "Nobes, you've got to help me. Mel threw me out of the Peppermint Lounge."

"How am I going to help you? I don't even know Mel."

"You're going to be my lawyer."

"Really?"

"Yeah, Mel threw me out and I told him I had a friend who was studying to be a lawyer at Harvard and I was going to bring him back with me."

"You have a friend that goes to Harvard?"

"Yeah you!"

Wow! I have a big ego, but Harvard and a lawyer? The only thing I knew about the law was that you should avoid getting caught. But this whole thing sounded interesting to me.

"Okay, I'm your Harvard lawyer. What do you want me to do?"

"I want you to get me back into the Peppermint Lounge."

Entrance to the Peppermint Lounge was important to certain types of individuals in those days. It was a very busy nightclub at Salisbury Beach. It was rock and roll and blues. I was strictly jazz. I went to the Peppermint Lounge occasionally but not often. I do remember seeing Fats

Domino in the parking lot by the entrance one night. He was sitting in a big car just beside the entrance door. He was swigging on a pint of Southern Comfort. There was a crowd of teenagers standing around his car. I had no idea who the fat man was. Somebody said, "That's Fats Domino." I said, "Well, you are right there. He sure is."

The Peppermint Lounge was just down a bit from the Salisbury Police Station and the public restrooms. It had a large dirt parking lot. It was also across the road from the roller coaster. Prior to being called the Peppermint Lounge it was Jenney's. A fellow named Mack Jenney or Mac Jenney owned it. For my friend Kibbi to be banned from this place this early in the season was a catastrophe. He was desperate. So I agreed to take his case.

As we walked down to the Peppermint Lounge Tom briefed me. I remember I was wearing a pair of Bermuda shorts. Everybody was wearing Bermuda shorts in those days. In addition I was wearing my multicolored Hawaiian Eye sport shirt and a pair of sandals. I kept asking myself if a Harvard lawyer would be dressed in this fashion. Why not? Harvard Lawyers must go to Salisbury Beach also.

Mel managed the Lounge. He was a short, fat, semi-bald guy who was always chewing a big cigar. He was an intimidating little fellow – picture Danny DiVito from *Taxi* and *My Cousin Vinnie*.

The case: Mel was going into the men's room as Kibbi was coming out. Upon entering the men's room Mel noticed the paper towel dispenser had been ripped from the wall. He turned around immediately; grabbed my buddy, Kibbi, and called one of his bouncers. Kibbi was then escorted to the exit and thrown bodily out onto the sidewalk.

My first question as a lawyer was, "Did you rip the paper towel dispenser from the wall, Tom?"

"Not exactly."

"Not exactly is not a good answer, Tom. There are only two correct answers to my question – yes I did or no I didn't."

"Listen Nobes, the thing was hanging there by one screw. I tried to pull a paper towel out of it and the damn thing falls off the wall. It could have happened to anybody. I just happened to be the wrong guy, in the wrong place, at the wrong time."

Humm! This was a Henry Fonda movie, wasn't it?

Man, my first case as a Harvard Lawyer and I have to get an obvious criminal. What would F. Lee Bailey do? I figured I'll have to do as real lawyers do – I'll baffle them with baloney.

I waited on the sidewalk while Kibbi tried to get back inside the club. The bouncer recognized him and wouldn't let him in. Kibbi demanded that the bouncer go and get Mel to come out and talk to his lawyer.

I figured this little game was all over. Mel wasn't going to come out and talk to some guy in Bermuda shorts and sporting a multicolored Hawaiian Eye shirt – the colors were pastels – pink, yellow, pale blue and turquoise.

But there he was.

I said, "You have accused my client here, Mr. Thomas Kabildis, of engaging in malicious, criminally destructive behavior."

"I don't have to talk to you," Mel said agitatedly while nervously attempting to eat his stubby cigar.

"Well, you can talk to me now, or you can talk to me in a court of law."

I couldn't believe it. We actually had Mel scared. Maybe I could really be a Harvard lawyer. It could happen!

Mel continued. "This guy ripped my towel machine off the wall. He has to pay for it."

"Did you see my client rip the towel machine off the wall?"

"No I didn't exactly see him, but he was the only one in there and the machine was laying on the bathroom floor."

"Really? You have nineteen million half drunk teenagers running in and out of your lavatory (note the use of the word lavatory), and just because you see my client leaving the room when you are entering, you accuse him of the crime? You have got to be making a joke.

"Tom, take a good look at this place because when I get done with this guy, it is all going to belong to you. This is deformation of character. This is slander. This is *identitae fraudulente*. People have collected millions on cases like this. This type of case was decided centuries ago. I think the first such case was at Nuremberg in 1346. It is what they call *no low expropriente*. We got this guy right where we want him. Let's go. We'll be seeing you in court, sir."

"Wait a minute, wait a minute. Listen I don't know all this Latin stuff and I don't want no court and legal problems. I'll let this guy back in this one last time but if I catch him doing anything he's going to be out of here for good."

"What do you think, Tom?"

"That's it? This guy accuses me of all these lies and I don't get anything? I should get something for being treated like this."

I looked at Mel. He was fidgeting and his cigar stub was bouncing every which way.

"Five free drinks," I said to Mel. He stared, pensively.

"One free drink," Mel countered.

"Three," I compromised.

"Two free drinks and that's my last offer."

"What do you say Kibbi?"

"Okay."

As Mel and Kibbi went strolling back inside and Kibbi joyfully bellied up to the bar I thought, Wow, I won my first case as a Harvard lawyer. Of course, it was pro-bono or maybe Sonny Bono, but a win is a win.

It's the Food, Stupid

It was a cold December night. A bunch of us had bundled up in a booth up at the Tally-ho. The Tally-ho was on Swan St. It had become a great place to hang out for the post high school and young adult crowd. Older folks came in too but they used the back entrance. They had a section of their own — away from the younger noisy bunch.

The Tally-ho was a sports bar before there was such a thing as a sports bar. There were TVs stationed appropriately in all the dining rooms and several at the bar. If anything was happening with Boston sports, it would be on the TVs at the Tally-ho. It was a great place to go to watch a Red Sox, Celtic or a Bruins game — lots of enthusiastic chums to cheer with. Paul Margraff was the owner/manager/bartender/waiter/sandwich maker during my era.

We were playing forty-fives at our booth. Forty-fives was a card game indigenous to Lawrence and the greater Merrimack Valley. Anyone I met in my travels who knew how to play the game of forty-fives had roots in the old neighborhood.

On this particular occasion an old buddy came walking through the door. We all looked up from our card game and recognized our old grammar school chum. In typical Lawrence fashion someone said, "Hey Billy, long time no see."

"Yeah, about 15 years."

"Has it been that long?"

"You've been gone 15 years? I didn't even know you had left town," offered another astute Lawrence observer at the table.

"Oh yeah, a little over 15 years now."

"Where have you been?"

"Well, all over but I settled in California for the last 10 years or so."

"Are you home for Christmas to see the relatives?"

"No, I'm back for good."

"You're back for good! What are you crazy? You finally get out of this town and you actually come back here to live? What are you nuts?"

Billy laughed. "Yeah, I suppose I am."

"No seriously, you were settled out there in beautiful California. You were there for 10 years, you say, and you come back to Lawrence? There has got to be something wrong. Somebody in the family must be sick or something?"

Billy laughed again. "No, not really. Everybody is doing fine. Just got a little homesick I guess."

Each of us at the card table dropped our hand and we all looked up at our old buddy.

Homesick was not a term many of us used in reference to Lawrence.

"You got homesick? What the heck could get anybody homesick for Lawrence? I know many people who said their home in Lawrence made them sick but I never heard anybody say that they were homesick for Lawrence. What could you possibly miss about Lawrence?"

"Well, guys like you for one thing. I kind of missed having four different seasons too. But I guess what I missed most of all about Lawrence was the food."

"The food! They don't have food in California?"

"They have food but nothing like the food we have here in Lawrence. No Tally-ho chicken bar-b-que, no Lawton's by the Sea deep-fried hot dogs, no Bea's cutlets, no Bishops, no Ceder Crest, no Bungalow, no Pappy's bakery, no anchovy or pepperoni crispellies. They never even heard of lemon slush or a Black Moon ice cream on a stick for cryin' out loud. Why, the homemade bread alone is worth the trip to Lawrence.

"There is a bakery on every corner around here. You want fresh baked Polish bread, you go down to Sunkist Bakery on Exchange St. You want Italian bread, you go down to Jackson or Common Streets. They have four bakeries at one intersection – one on each corner down there. You want French bread, you've got it. You have home baked Syrian bread everywhere. You have German restaurants, French restaurants, Syrian restaurants, Italian restaurants, and Chinese Restaurants. Even the diners around here are great – the Broadway Diner, Ritzie's, Jubert's, Falon's, the Post Office Diner with Rudy, Ernie's Diner and Mushy's famous baked beans.

"I have been dreaming about a homemade pastry square for years. Where else can you get fresh backed fig squares, raisin squares, lemon tarts and Napoleons? I bought an Italian meat pie up on Broadway at P.J.'s the other day. You can't find a meat pie like that anywhere in America but Lawrence. Thawites and Fould's French pork pies, hot or cold – a little ketchup and you're in business. I've never seen a pie like that any place but here. Kibbi and shish kabob sandwiches, Tripoli and Christy's home-style Italian pizza, Essem hot dogs and Polish kielbasa, Barrett's tomato sausage – you guys are all used to it. You take it all for granted. But let me tell you, they don't have food like this in other places."

"So you will put up with ten feet of snow and a million people huddled in tenement houses for a homemade cruller or jelly donut? You're easy."

32

"Yeah, that's what the girls always said. Hey, I was raised in a tenement house. There are worse places to live than a tenement house. Tenement houses don't make slums – people do. When I was coming up around here we had no central heat or air-conditioning. We didn't even have hot water. If you wanted a bath you had to heat the kettles up on the stove. Now all these tenements got heat, air, hot water – what the hell?"

Mr. Danny Tardugno, a little gray haired fellow who worked behind the bar at the Tally-ho for years, called out Billy's sandwich order.

"You better go get those sandwiches, Billy, before the Tally-ho stops making burgers."

"Yeah, like that's ever goin' to happen. Take care guys. I'll see ya the next time I get hungry."

"Good enough pal."

Murder and Big, Bad Billy Quinlan

Everyone knows the poet Robert Frost graduated from Lawrence High School. In reading a biography about Mr. Frost he was quoted as stating that one of his biggest regrets was that he never wrote a history of Lawrence, Massachusetts. At the time that I read this statement I was not familiar with the history of Lawrence and I wondered why a great and famous man like Robert Frost would want to write a history of my rather abused and rundown hometown. Now that I am a little more familiar with the history of Lawrence, I understand his regret.

I started reading Robert Frost because he was from Lawrence and over the years I have kept my eye open for other famous people from Lawrence.

Leonard Bernstein was in my little apartment living room in Lawrence every Sunday for quite a while. Of course he appeared there via my oval-screened Zenith television set. I think Leonard started coming to my house around the year 1954. He had a series of programs where he explained the roots of music. It was truly a great series. I remember rushing home from King Tut's – I mean church – every Sunday just to watch Leonard. I'm sure he was trying to get me interested in classical music. He was not successful. He did succeed in getting me interested in Leonard Bernstein and music in general.

Leonard Bernstein was born in Lawrence. His father had a little bookstore on the corner of Amesbury and Essex Street. I bought books at that shop. I remember ordering a copy of Plato's Symposium. The poor man running the shop at that time (early 1960s) had to purchase 4 copies. I bought one and the other three are probably still sitting there. If you are interested in getting a copy of Plato's Symposium, they are on the left side of the store on a shelf at about eye level. They have a yellow cover. I was told the shop is still in business.

Ed McMahon was raised in Lowell. He had his first broadcasting job at WLLH. Ed told a story on the Johnny Carson Show about how he used to be the guess-your-weight-guy at Salisbury Beach.

I remember him! He had his stand just to the left of the Frolics heading towards the 5 O'clock Club. That was a great game. Ed would agree to guess the year of your car or your mother's first name or your age or a million other things. If he happened to get it right or within a year, or whatever the caveat was, you got no prize for your dollar or your quarter. But if he guessed wrong you won a prize off the dollar shelf or the quarter shelf or whatever your wager. People often won. But even if you won you lost. If you bet a dollar and picked a prize from the dollar shelf, the prize was probably worth a quarter or less. Everybody realized this but people still played the game. I played it too. A lot of it had to do with the Ed McMahons at the stand and their style.

Just think I may have contributed to Ed McMayon's success. But let me say I had nothing to do with his recent bankruptcy. Ed took my dollar and he blew it. What can I say?

Then there is Jay Leno who grew up in Andover. I really don't know anything about Jay. I don't think I've watched the Johnny Carson show since Johnny retired. I still consider Jay an "upstart." I have recently read he got a

35

boost up on his road to fame and fortune by talking Lennie of Lennie's on the Turnpike into featuring a stand up comedian along side all that jazz out on route 1 for the first time in the club's history. I frequented Lennie's in those days but never saw Jay – or don't remember seeing him if I did.

Robert Goulet was born in Lawrence. I have a friend who says he knew Robert and played with him when they were children. But my friend has been known to lie. He told me Robert lived in the projects "over the other side" of Essex Street. I have been to all sides of Essex St. but still haven't been able to determine which is "the other side."

But now here is a story that is true. Billy Quinlan and I were involved in a life and death struggle one night. He was very much alive and I thought I was dead.

I was cruising by the Merry Mac Club up on the river road one evening. I didn't have much money. In fact, I had enough for one drink – no tip for the bartender. I was a "social" drinker at the time. Most of my friends were also "social" drinkers. Many of us today are having a little problem with our livers. I am wondering if this has anything to do with the drinking water in Lawrence. After all, those mixed drinks were 90% Lawrence water. I have been thinking of investigating and possibly of starting up a class action suit. I know for a fact cirrhosis of the liver is prevalent in Lawrence. I would not be surprised if it is disproportional to the rest of the nation. I may look into this after I finish this project. Then again maybe I won't.

So I took up a stool at the bar at the Merry Mac Club. I was sipping my drink and minding my own business when this fellow next to me started a conversation. We chatted. As it turned out he had an interest in classic philosophy – me too. We discussed Plato and Aristotle for awhile and then moved on to St. Thomas Aquinas and then into the Reformation. The night lingered along and every time I

36

came back from the bathroom, there was another drink waiting for me. I figured this red-headed, Irish fellow I had been talking to was my benefactor. He was most likely fascinated by my intellect.

I thanked him each time and we moved on. By the time we got to Bertrand Russell, Jean Paul Sartre and Martin Heidegger, the lights began to flash and the Merry Mac Club was in shutdown mode. I sloshed down my last drink, shook hands with my red-headed philosopher buddy, thanked him for his kindness and started for the door.

A voice from behind me then bellowed, "Hey you! You're not going to leave without buying me a drink, are you?" I turned and there was Big Bad Billy Quinlan leaning on the bar.

Billy was a professional football player from 1957 to 1965. He played for several pro teams – the Cleveland Browns, the Green Bay Packers, Detroit and some others. He had a reputation as the dirtiest, toughest player in professional football. He was born in Lawrence and he had a Lawrence reputation also.

After retiring from professional football he bought a barroom on Common St. Everybody liked Billy but if Billy didn't like you – you could soon be looking for a new body.

At the time of this story Billy's name had been in the Eagle Tribune. He had an altercation with some Mafia gangster types at a Holiday Inn. If I remember the story correctly he threw one of the bad guys through a plate glass window and put a few of the others into the hospital – all of which was determined to be self-defense as I recall.

"Are you talking to me?" I said.

I didn't say the above in Robert De Nero fashion as in Taxi Driver. I would imagine I sounded more like Woody Allen – rather wimpy and terrified.

"Yeah, I'm talkin' to you. I've been buying you drinks all damn night and you ain't bought me one. What's the story?"

The place went quiet. The owner John McGrath was behind the bar. He was a big guy too. I thought he was my buddy. He wasn't leaping in my support. I thought of running. I could run away from a professional football player? I don't think so. I could fall to the floor and play dead? Or, I could just stand there for a few more minutes and be dead.

"Ah, I ah … Red here has been buying my drinks." Red shook his head negatively and confirmed the allegations by Big Bad Billy. "Well, I ah … maybe …" What could I do? I had no money. I shouldn't have been there and I never should have accepted all those drinks. I stood there stuttering for what seemed to be at least a year, when my buddy Billy Quinlan finally spoke again.

"Oh screw you," he said. Then he turned and headed out the door.

So there you go … how I met the infamous Lawrence professional football star Billy Quinlan.

Hey Billy, if you are still out there, I have a little more money today than I did in those days. I'd love to buy you a drink. Unfortunately, I have been advised not to drink alcohol by several different physicians. I think it's the Lawrence water. Are you having any trouble with your liver, Billy? What do you think about the water in Lawrence?

The Old Gang and Our First Cottage

Up until the age of sixteen my folks always tried to get the family off for a week or two "at the beach" every year. At sixteen "the gang" took over. The old gang rented a cottage at the beach every year from the time I was 16 until I reached the age of 27. We had a few guys who were old enough to sign the leases in our early days. But as I remember there were many rental owners who were not all that particular. If you had the money, you got the cottage.

I think we had 40 guys who chipped in for our first all season rental at Hampton Beach. The cottage was called the Marilyn and it was on Island Path. This particular cottage is notorious in the minds of our original renters to this day.

Every evening the floors were littered with bodies. The beds went to the original seven or eight of us who thought up this timeshare idea. On several weekends even the floors would be filled. The bodies then spilled over into the cars in the tiny parking lot.

I remember coming in late and stepping over people to get to my bedroom. When I stepped on somebody and they voiced their disapproval, my response was rather Reaganesque, "Hey listen you, I'm one of the guys who is paying for this place!" The person lying on the floor would usually apologize. It was often necessary to evict strangers from my bed. For the most part they respected their position and found a new spot on the floor.

The Marilyn was down the end of a road and surrounded by a swamp. The cottage was isolated by the swamp which added a certain amount of privacy and mysteriousness to it. The swamp was kept at bay by a large wooden fence. The cottage was really a shack. It leaned to one side. We didn't know if it was sinking into the swamp or just falling over.

The Marilyn was well known to the Hampton Beach Police Department. Most of the cops on the force had been to our home away from home so many times, that we actually befriended a number of them. When a cruiser happened to appear outside our little paradise by the sea, someone would go to the window and then announce whether the officers were friend or foe. If the officer was foe, we usually got a warning about the noise or the loud music and were told to calm it down. Kids like us were important to the beach economic community – for a while at least.

Our little villa by the swamp gained a reputation and became a must-go-to place for the junior crowd. We had guests from all walks of society.

On one occasion an overdressed young man came in with his equally over-dressed girlfriend. The young man knew one of our forty renters and just happened to be in the area. They were gawkers and obviously slumming. The young lady was wide-eyed and clearly astounded. The young man was proud as a peacock to be able to show his date this underside of life. Their faces beamed and their eyes rolled around wide and astonished. Clearly they had never seen anything like this before in their lives. I imagine to their minds it was much like a trip to New York's infamous Bowery or skid row.

Things were going well until a cruiser pulled up outside. One of our full-timers peeked out a window. He turned and gave the "no problem" signal. Our uptown guests, unfortunately, were not familiar with our signals. The young man went to the window and took a peek for himself. He exploded, "It's the police!"

He and his local prom queen began rushing around in every direction. We all sat watching them curiously. Hadn't they ever seen a police cruiser or a cop before? What was with this couple?

By the time our two buddies from the Hampton Beach Police Department came to the door. Rodney and Penelope (not their real names) had vanished.

We all chatted with the cops. They gave us the usual warning about not letting things get out of hand and then they left.

A short time passed and we all began to wonder where our two well dressed tourists had disappeared to. Someone recalled seeing them scurrying out the back door. We wandered out back. We heard some whimpering. It was coming from the swamp-side of the fence. We hiked one of the boys up to take a peek over the fence. There, waist deep in muck and mire, sat our two new friends, Rodney and Penelope.

We lowered them a rope and somehow pulled them both from the soggy, snake ridden mire. He did not look good. She looked much worse. They went home. They had their fill of skid row and the Bowery Boys.

Our season ended abruptly at the Marilyn when we all returned from the Center one evening and found a sign on our front door. Our cottage had been condemned. We weren't even allowed back inside to claim our "valuables." We thought briefly that our rights had been violated and maybe we could sue somebody. But then on second thought, we decided we best leave well enough alone.

Okay Boys, Back Off and Spread Out!

A Summer with Charlie is a rather short book. It is actually a long short story. While writing it I tried to keep the focus of the book on Charlie and his life situation and not get lost recording the various antics of the infamous Howard Ass – as Ray Dolan had dubbed the old corner gang. Consequently there was more left out of the book about that fateful summer than actually went into the book. Here's one that didn't make the cut.

After a rather ruckus weekend at Old Towne Way and everybody had disappeared back to the city and the real world of 9 to 5, Charlie and I were left to clean up the disaster. Charlie relished this duty. I don't know why. But he would scurry around in his pork pie hat and bathing suit with broom or mop in hand whistling and humming all morning. I suppose if I didn't have such a terrible hangover every Monday morning, I would have found this comforting rather than annoying.

The first thing we discovered was somebody had broken the commode in our unique back porch toilet.

The bathroom sat on the back porch of our cottage. Hang a right after exiting the kitchen, take about fifteen paces and there was a door. The average homeowner would probably conclude the door to this shelter hid a utility room or a storage closet, but it contained the toilet and a bathroom sink.

Being rather unhandy, I was under the impression commodes were another of those mysteries provided by God in his infinite goodness – a divine intervention of sorts. Commodes always were and always would be, thank-you God, amen.

That is not the case. Commodes are man-made. Right there in this little hardware store in the town of Salisbury sat a variety of commodes for sale.

We installed the new commode and put the old one on the back porch a few paces from the kitchen door. We would take it to the dump with all the empty beer, wine and hard liquor bottles the Monday following this weekend's fiasco.

For this weekend's agenda we had a new idea – we would concoct a "punch" for the girls. Girls dig punch and we figured it would add an air of class to the joint. Besides, everybody was drinking up all the Seagram's 7, Smirnoff Vodka, Bacardi Rum, Beefeater Gin and our prized Kruger beer in the little ugly Kruger bottles.

The more we thought about this punch the more involved it got. We wanted to put a large amount of hard liquor in our punch, of course. Girls need a good shot or two before they can loosen up. But girls are also very cautious. They don't want to get too loose – which means the potency of the punch has to be disguised in some way or other. Then there was the expense. We always had lots of company and strangers can suck up a good quantity of free punch.

We bought several quart bottles of booze that came under the Shamrock logo. Shamrock? It was about a quarter the price of any booze that was for real. It was horrible, but we had a plan.

We bought one quart of Shamrock scotch, one quart of Shamrock gin, one quart of Shamrock rum, one quart of Shamrock vodka, and one quart of Shamrock Irish whiskey. But now we needed something to make all this

43

booze taste like Kool-aide. We bought two gallons of sweet Cucamonga wine, several large cans of fruit cocktail and various other fruits, a few cans of Dole pineapple rings to float on the top, and six large cans of Hawaiian Punch. I suppose in today's world this could be construed to be the original date rape drug.

We went to a used kitchen supply store and got a bunch of "punch glasses" for about two cents each. They weren't very dainty. They were all different colors and had nice handles on them but they probably held a full cup of liquid each. We thought one cup per dip of punch was just about right.

We couldn't find the right sized punchbowl though. Then somebody suggested we use the kitchen sink. It was a good sized, old-fashioned, deep, dishwashing sized sink. What a great idea!

Shortly before things got rolling that Saturday night we prepared the sink for the punch. A few of the guys used the sink that morning to shave. Consequently there were a ton of little hairs sticking to the white porcelain bowl. We had nine guys and only one bathroom – some facial hair in the kitchen sink was to be expected. We cleaned it – a little. We bought new sink stoppers and made sure the sink did not leak. We didn't want all our efforts washing down the drain.

We dumped all the booze into the kitchen sink punch bowl and then gradually added Cucamonga wine, canned fruit and Hawaiian Punch until the taste of the Shamrock liquor was undetectable. That took all the Hawaiian Punch, all the Cucamonga wine, and all the canned fruit. The canned fruit and the floating pineapple rings did add a very nice touch.

When the girls started wandering in, it was mandatory that they be escorted by one of the house "chaperones" over to the sink for a try at the punch. [We thought of ourselves more as guardian angels than as chaperones.]

All the girls loved the punch. It was so sweet and "yummy."

"Is there much liquor in here?" she would ask, naively.

"Noooo, it is mostly fruit and Hawaiian Punch," one of us cottage angels would advise.

Well, I am gonna tell you, the girls loosened up pretty quick after a couple of "tiny" cups of that hobo style Hawaiian Punch.

The first cup would only be a quarter full for most girls. But after awhile they wound be stumbling over one another to that sink laughing, giggling and slopping up those cups to the brim. By the fourth or fifth cup of Hobo Punch the girls were bobbing for fruit cocktail cherries and getting pineapple rings caught on their noses.

Actually we had overdone it. A few hours at our punch bowl and most of the girls weren't good for anything — even a little idle conversation was difficult.

For example, me and Charlie were cooling off out on the back porch having a cigarette. The interior of the cottage was jammed. A girl suddenly came tumbling out the kitchen door. She looked like she could have been a very nice girl before she found the Hobo Punch. She was quite pretty — in a drunken, disheveled sort of way. She had long brown hair and was wearing a pair of tight, butt-hugging jeans. She wobbled there for a minute doing her best to stand erect and remain in one place.

"Rough sea tonight, huh sailor?" Charlie commented with a bemused grin.

"F'in right it is," she slurred. "And if I don't pee pretty quick there's going to be an ocean of trouble right here in river city." At that moment she glanced to her right and saw the old commode sitting on the porch. "God," she exclaimed. "This is a classy joint! But what the hell! When in Rome as they F'in say. Okay boys, back off and spread out!"

She stepped up – or backed up – to the commode, unbuttoned her pants, pulled down her drawers, sat on the commode and peed with a big sigh of relief. When she finished she looked around desperately. Then beamed up at Charlie and me and said. "Fellas, I can take an F'in joke but where the hell is the toilet paper?"

We both looked at her and pointed. "It's in the bathroom just behind that door," we chimed.

She took a gander down to her right towards the bathroom door, then shook her head and mumbled in frustration. "You have got to be shi----g me!"

"Honey please, you are talking to the clean up crew," Charlie said crushing his Lucky Strike on the deck. "A little pee on the back porch is acceptable but any more than that and you're cleaning it up yourself, matey."

Forty-Fives

Everyone in Lawrence is born knowing how to play the card game 45's. I figure that must be the case because I can remember learning everything else but not 45's.

Johnny Bolton taught me how to smoke and inhale. Frankie Spires and his mom and dad across the way on Chelmsford St. taught me how to play canasta, gin rummy, and hearts. Bobby Scott taught me how to shoot marbles. The Moffet brothers taught me how to play scalars — a game played by tossing baseball cards up against a wall or somebody's stoop. My Uncle Ray taught me how to ride a bicycle. The St. John brothers taught me how to steal things from Woolworth 5 and 10 on Essex St. I won't name the individual who introduced me to my first bottle of Black Horse Ale or the Narragansett GIQ but I know who he was. And a girl named Barbara taught me ... well, I don't think I'll go there just now. But I can't remember anybody teaching me how to play 45's. I think I always knew how. It was just there in the genes.

Anyone I ever met in my travels hobo-ing around America or otherwise who confessed to knowing how to play 45's came from Merrimack Valley — most often Lawrence.

Forty-fives was more than a card game though. It was in the skill or craft category. There were numerous rules to the game but more important were the unwritten rules.

The unwritten rules all related to what card one should have played instead of what one, in his or her ignorance, did end up playing.

One of the problems with this book of unwritten rules is that everyone had a different book of unwritten rules. Playing 45's partners was very popular. But invariably husbands and wives never seemed to have the same book of unwritten rules.

Common phrases heard around the 45's card table were: Honey, it is just common sense; Everybody knows that, sugarplum; Why baby, why; Can I have a new partner next game?

Exchanging mates in a game of 45's partners was the closest anybody came to wife swapping in Lawrence, Massachusetts in my time.

When men played partners, the phrases changed in intensity and style but the intent was the same.

In mulling this game over in my mind today, I think the golden rule of the game was: It doesn't matter how you play the game as long as you argue like hell after each hand and abuse your partner until she leaves the table crying or he challenges you to step outside and settle this like a man.

On the corner somebody always had a deck of cards and we played this game hour, after hour, after hour.

Me, Jack Sheehy, Frank Duchnowski and a few other close buddies loved this game so much that even as drinking age adults we often opted out of a night on the nightclub circuit to go to the Immaculate Conception Church cellar or the cafeteria at St. Rita's School for a Card Party (that's Caahhd Paahhdy). There was a small fee to get into the Party. The proceeds went to the missions, the church furnace fund or directly to the Pope in Rome. He had a furnace fund also.

The entrance fee didn't really matter to us guys because we were there to win and advance the reputation of the younger generation and of the Howard Associates (Howard Ass for short). It did not matter how old or feeble the folks were at St. Rita's cafeteria if they sat at one of our tables, they had best be ready to lose.

What I remember most about the St. Rita's and Immaculate Conception 45's card parties was that no matter how sweet, friendly or pious looking these old people were, no matter the holy artifacts pinned to their clothing or hanging around their necks, they all cheated. Everyone cheated. Every game ended up 145 to 115. These were the highest possible winning and losing scores.

I don't really remember how they figured out at the end of the night who got the prizes. I think they drew names out of a hat. But I do remember me and my buddies often won.

The first place prize was either an 11 lb. Krakus brand, Polish canned ham or a gift certificate for a fresh 20 lb turkey from the Park St. Food Bank (formally Adolph's Variety) or Catalano's Market on Common St. Second and third prizes were an entire boxful of donated canned goods – 2 cans of Chef Boyardee Ravioli, 4 cans of Campbell's Tomato Soup, a large box of LUX soap powder, a box of Ritz Crackers and four 1000 sheet rolls of Scott toilet paper.

I think they often picked me and my buddies out as the winners for two reasons. Letting us win sucked us young blood in for next Monday night's card party and we always re-donated the prizes. That, of course, meant next week's prizes were ready to roll and the Pope got the money for the steam heat at the Vatican without even paying a vigorish.

Sure, they all may have cheated but they were good Catholics nevertheless.

The Banana Boat

We dubbed my 1946 fluid drive DeSoto, the Banana Boat. It was very big and very yellow. It was a beauty. It looked like something out of an old Mafia Prohibition movie. The backseat doors opened from the wrong side. It had a clutch but you didn't have to use it if you didn't want to. It had tiny, rounded windows. It was heavy duty and weighed as much as a military tank.

Trying to navigate through Methuen Square was perilous – not for me but for everybody else. The windows were like tiny ship portholes. Peripheral vision was not good.

I would sneak across Broadway then barrel up that hill leading into Methuen Square. It was a full stop at the top of the hill. But stopping did me no good. I could never see anything. I would simply hit the horn about halfway up the hill, hold my breath and floor it right on through that five way intersection. On occasion I would hear the screeching of breaks and horns blasting. But after a year or so I think everybody recognized the Banana Boat and took appropriate action.

I hit a telephone pole with it and did considerable damage to the pole. I couldn't find anything damaged on the car.

The Banana Boat was my first car and my Uncle Ray helped me get it. My Uncle Ray was a very precautionary and meticulous fellow. He had a method for doing everything. He even had a system for shoveling snow. I won't get into it today. It is a little too complicated for my average reader. It involves some calculus and a good deal of analytic geometry.

Uncle Ray instructed me on the multiple and many hazards and responsibilities of car ownership. That the seller only wanted $10 and a ride to the airport for the classic '46 DeSoto was of minor importance compared to the expenses of proper tire rotation, inspection fees and regular servicing, my Uncle Ray advised. Car ownership was a grave responsibility and Uncle Ray explained it all to me in great detail.

As it turned out I drove the Banana Boat for a number of years and never spent a nickel on anything. I tried to get it tuned up once but the mechanic couldn't get the spark plugs out of it. He said, "I think the plugs are welded to the head. Drive it until it dies, save your money and go buy a real car."

The Banana Boat served us well for a few seasons at both Hampton and Salisbury Beach. It provided many an enjoyable evening at the Den Rock Drive-in Theater. It also got me, Jack Sheehy, Barry Curtin and Dick Pansella through our first year at Northern Essex Community College in Haverhill.

After the spark plug incident the radiator sprung a leak. We carried gallon jugs of water in the trunk. Then the starter developed a bad spot. Wherever we went, the Banana Boat had to be parked on a hill. When the tubes (remember tire tubes?) started popping through the treads, I found a new old tire and threw it on.

I got to NECC early every day and parked the Banana Boat at the top of the grade around the corner. When we left each evening we had a cheering section. With the doors all held open, my three passengers would push. When we rounded the corner and started rolling down the

51

hill, I'd pop the clutch and broommm, we were off. Everybody would run and jump in (like on an Olympic bobsled run) and we would all wave out the windows to our fans as we jerked and stuttered off.

I suppose the onlookers found this amusing. I never thought about it and I don't ever remember any of my passengers bringing it up. We all considered it usual and customary – after all, we were from Lawrence. We considered all the other students waving and laughing as an impromptu fan club of sorts. They obviously admired us for our ingenuity. And why not!

When we got back to Lawrence, I would drop Barry and Rick off at their homes. Me and Jack would park the Banana Boat at the Howard on the hill on Birchwood Road. It would stay parked there all night and every night waiting for its "students" to return in the morning.

Each morning, all the way from Lawrence to Haverhill, Barry Curtin would keep us entertained relating conversations he had with his mother the previous evening. Barry had a way with words. He spoke rather coarsely back then. Every third word was the "F" word. I am sure Barry is a CFO somewhere today and his speech is much more sophisticated.

"So what did your mother say last night Barry?"

"Oh man was she ever F'in pissed! She said, 'Barry Curtin, you little F'in snot, if you waste all my F'in money on this F'in college crap and you don't become the F'in president of something when you F'in grow up, I'm gonna kick your F'in butt all over this F'in kitchen. You better learn F'in something. I never see you studying any F'in books or writing any F'in crap in any of your F'in notebooks. I looked in one of them F'in notebooks last night and there ain't one F'in note in the whole F'in thing. Are you doing anything at that F'in college or are you doin' the same F'in thing you always do ... F'in nothing'.' God was she ever pissed. I've got to start F'in studying and

52

get something beside an F'in D or she is going to F'in disown me. It was bad last night man – really F'in bad."

I learned, 40 years later, Butchy Mall and some of his little buddies from the Howard Ass Junior Associates used to jumpstart the Banana Boat parked up at the Howard some nights and go joyriding. I really didn't mind that, but the little buggers could have put a gallon of gas in it every now and then. I thought the gas tank was leaking. I put a pan underneath it each night to catch the gas but there was never a puddle anywhere. I couldn't figure where to move the damn pan. Those little squirts!

The Cedar Crest Restaurant

The Cedar Crest was a diner on one side and a sit-down family restaurant on the other. It was a neat place. As a child I ate there only once. My family didn't have much money and we didn't eat out often. In fact, that one meal we had at the Cedar Crest is the only childhood dining out experience I can remember. My father who had been working as a Merchant Marine finally got a local job working at the new Merit gas station on Broadway across from the Arlington Mill. It was a big event. My father hated going off to sea. To find local employment was monumental. He wanted to give us all a treat. We got spiffied up in our Sunday clothes and we were off to the Cedar Crest.

I got fried chicken. After I finished my chicken the waitress brought me a bowl. The bowl had lemons floating in it. My mother often made me a drink with lemons in it when I was sick with a cold. I couldn't understand why they had put my hot lemon drink in a bowl as opposed to a cup. I picked it up with both hands and started to drink it. It wasn't hot and it wasn't sweet. The waitress leaned over and whispered in my ear, "You don't drink it, honey. You wash your fingers in it."

As workingmen me and my two buddies, Jack Sheehy and Frank Duchnowski ate in the diner side of the Cedar Crest often. We would meet there after work. We even had a favorite waitress. She became our favorite because of one incident.

We had rushed in at supper time after cleaning somebody's cellar or something. The waitress brought our menus. We each picked up a menu and she stopped instantly. "What have you guys been doing?" she asked. We each looked at one another curiously. What did she care what we were doing? "Well, it doesn't really matter what you've been doing. You guys ain't ordering anything until you get into that bathroom and wash your hands."

"What are you my mother?" Dutchy protested.

"Don't give me none of that. Get into that bathroom and wash your hands or it's no supper for any of you."

The three of us looked at each other. Dutch shrugged, then got up and headed for the bathroom, mumbling – me and Jack followed.

I guess we liked the personal attention because we asked for that waitress from then on. When she came to our table we would all hold out our hands for her inspection. She would nod her approval and then take our orders. I must admit, I thought Dutch would fail inspection on many of those occasions.

My last visit to the Cedar Crest was a long time coming. I had been gone from Lawrence for at least 20 years. My wife and I decided to give the old hometown a tour and look up some relatives. I had this rather strange aunt. My father used to say she had the first penny she ever earned. We called her and she suggested a meeting at the Cedar Crest for lunch. "The prices are cheaper at lunch time, you know," she advised.

We met outside the restaurant on Broadway. My aunt immediately headed for the diner side of the restaurant. "No, no," I said. "This is a special occasion. Let's celebrate and eat in the fancy side." Again she warned that on the fancy side the prices were higher. It took some persuading but finally she surrendered.

We had a surprisingly good time. I got the oven roast beef. My wife got the pot roast. I hadn't had an oven roast beef in years. Everything was great. Unfortunately there was no waitress checking the cleanliness of our hands, but it still felt like home. We discussed the "good old days" and then we were off.

I would like to eat at the Cedar Crest one more time but I'm afraid it won't happen. Either I will be gone or it will be gone before too long. But it was certainly fun while it lasted.

And, by the way, that rich aunt of mine died and left over a million dollars to her surviving brothers and sisters. Twenty thousand trickled down to me and the wife and helped finance an adventure we called "Hobo's Ice Cream Parlor."

We sold Hobo's for four time what we paid for it and it is the profits from that adventure which has supplied the capital for this book – and all my other books.

I feel I shouldn't let this opportunity go by without thanking my dad's dreaded, penny-pinching younger sister, Dorothy Noble, a lifetime AT&T telephone operator.

The Den Rock Drive-in

The Den Rock drive-in theater was on route 114 before the Den restaurant and past McGovern's roadside eatery.

The drive-in movie was one of those 60's things. I suppose there is now a whole generation who has no idea what a drive-in movie was – like a 45 record or 33 and 1/3 vinyl record album or 8 track tape. But the drive-in movie was better than all of those things. Talk about a big screen. The drive-in movie was the biggest screen ever. It was bigger than any movie theater. It was bigger than a highway billboard. It was big.

You sat and watched this giant movie screen from the comfort of your automobile. I imagine some married folks took their kids to a drive-in but it was primarily a teenager thing to our generation. It was a meeting, greeting, drinking, dating, hangout thing. In fact, if you were born in the late 60's or 70's there is a good chance you were conceived at a drive-in movie.

Many parents were aware of what went on sexually at drive-in movies and would not let their daughters accept a date to a drive-in movie. Strangely enough parents would let their daughters go to the drive-in with other girls. So cars full of girls would file in with cars full of boys bumping up behind them. Once inside the movie the cars would empty and then the passengers would rearrange themselves with the different sexes intermingling.

Boys and girls both would leave their vehicles and go "wandering." Their goal was either to find somebody or be found by somebody.

One excuse for wandering was the refreshment stand. They would interrupt the movie periodically and play an ad for the refreshment stand. They played a little promotional jingle that was also enticing. "We're going to the lobby; we're going to the lobby; we're going to the lobby; to get ourselves a treat." They would show on the screen little cartoon characters marching joyously off to the refreshment stand. It looked like such fun we all just had to do it. Actually it was fun.

The food at the stand was all pre-prepared and wrapped or packaged in aluminum keep-hot bags. Nothing I can remember was of a five star quality. But they had subs, hot dogs, hamburgers, meatball sandwiches, French fries, pizza slices, candy, popcorn, soda, coffee, cigarettes and whatever.

Underage boys also hunted older booze buyers and then would go to the drive-in to drink and party.

Metal poles held the speakers. Each car would have an individual speaker to pipe the sound into their auto.

Unfortunately for the drive-in theater owners, sneaking into a drive-in became a sport. The customary practice was to hide as many kids in the trunk as possible. Two passengers in the front seat looked cool. A boy and a girl in the front seat was a sure thing and two girls was good. Two boys was a little embarrassing but usually got by.

One evening, me and a bunch of my buddies had gotten all of our goodies, gathered. We stopped at McGovern's parking lot to draw straws and see who was going into the trunk. But when we tabulated all our capital, we only had enough for one fare. One boy driving a vehicle into a drive-in movie was not the best tactic – very suspicious. But we had no choice. Since it was my 1946 DeSoto fluid drive we were going in, I was elected the designated driver. I had a big trunk but on this occasion we had so many guys going into the trunk that they were nervous about locking the trunk completely – they didn't want to become "asphyxiated."

They all piled into the trunk and the last guy in held the trunk open slightly. I was to give them a warning shortly before we pulled in, at which point they would slam the trunk and lock it.

I anticipated a long line getting into the movie. I didn't want the guys stuffed in the trunk to be locked in there too long. I decided to wait until just before I was pulling in to announce my warning. Just as I was crossing the highway leading up to the entrance, I slapped my left hand on the outside of the driver's door and to make double sure they heard me I yelled out the window, "Okay, we're pulling in."

I heard the trunk slam. But no sooner did the trunk slam than there was a cop standing in my driveway. He had his hands on his hips and a very unhealthy look on his face. I came to a stop without hitting him. He slowly walked around my vehicle. When he finally ended up by the driver's window I looked up. With my well rehearsed and practiced poker face I said. "Yes officer? Something wrong?"

He bent over and stuck his head in my little window. He glowed his flashlight, exploring my backseat. He pulled back up to a standing position and folded his arms across his chest. With a slight smirk he said, "Going to the movies by yourself, son?"

"Yeah," I said. "My girlfriend's sick and I really wanted to see this movie."

"What's the name of the movie tonight?" he asked, cynically.

"I stammered and stuttered and tried to see the billboard out the corner of my eye."

"Okay son," he said losing his smirk. "Turn this tub around and get the hell out of here."

"Yes sir."

By the time I got back to McGovern's the guys in the trunk were screaming bloody murder. But I couldn't stop the car on the highway or where the cop could still see me. Right? What the heck!

Nobody died. But the "trunk people" weren't happy with me for a long, long time. Not happy at all.

Walter's Variety

Walter owned a little variety store on the corner of Center and Willow in North Lawrence. It was one block over and just down the hill from the Howard Playground on Lawrence St.

Walter would let us little guys hang out at his place. This was greatly appreciated in those cold winter months. We always knew Walter "loved" us little guys but, nevertheless, his patience had its limits. Periodically we'd hear a scream, "Okay boy's, on your way – time to clear the house here."

"But Walter, it's still snowing outside," we would whine.

"And so it is. On your way! Go to the boy's club or someplace."

"Let's go up to Clifford's."

Clifford was another case entirely. We had to buy something in order to be allowed to sit in Clifford's Ice Cream Parlor. So as we dragged up the hill to the corner of Lawrence and Chelmsford through the cold wind and driving show, we would all start counting our pennies. Six or seven of us would pile into a booth and one or two of us would order a hot chocolate. His hot chocolate was only a dime. He would top off the hot chocolate with a little spoonful of vanilla ice cream. We could take a long time drinking the hot chocolate using the excuse that it was too hot to drink quickly.

Occasionally he would play his organ for us. We really didn't care much for his organ playing but if we gave a loud enough cheer he would continue playing and we would get to stay inside and soak up more heat. He had a fancy Gulbranson's deluxe model organ.

"Wow, that was great Mr. Clifford. Do you know any more songs?"

"How about this one," and off he would go.

The next evening we would be back to good old Walter's Variety. By then Walter would have reconsidered his impatience of the previous evening and everything would once again be hunky-dory. But nevertheless there would come an evening when Walter would get sick of us and we would be off to Clifford's to get a ten cent hot chocolate.

One day Walter asked a bunch of us if he established hot chocolate and ice cream at his variety store would we buy from him instead of Clifford? Why of course we would we told him. We thought he was just jealous and needed to be reassured.

Within a week or two Walter's Variety was under construction. We kids could not believe our eyes – or ears for that matter. What was Walter doing?

Walter actually built a complete soda fountain out of the front portion of his storage room. It was beautiful, complete with ice cream cases, shake machines and a barrel that sat on the counter flashing a sign that boasted "Hot Chocolate." The hot chocolate sign waved back and forth on the top of a big hot chocolate barrel.

It was a great idea but none of us kids really had much money. We only bought hot chocolate at Clifford's because Clifford would not let us stay inside out of the cold unless we bought something. It was always warm and cozy inside Walter's. At Walter's we could get our traditional bag of Granite State potato chips and a C&J unique soda of our choice. Curran and Joyce (C&J) offered unique flavors like orange phosphate, sarsaparilla, lime rickey and more. Who needed a hot chocolate?

For weeks at closing time Walter would come storming into the soda fountain where we would all be sitting and grab that barrel of steaming hot chocolate and pour it down the drain.

"Gee Walter, if you are just going to dump all the hot chocolate down the drain, why don't you give each of us a free cup? It ain't right to just waste it like that."

For a long time Walter simply ignored our pleas. His face would get a little red and he sometimes stuttered a little, but nothing intelligible dribbled out. We couldn't understand it. Walter was usually very generous hearted.

One night as we all leaned over the counter and watched Walter pour the hot chocolate down the drain, he exploded.

"You guys drive me nuts! I pay good money to put in this whole soda fountain and buy this hot chocolate maker and I don't think one of you guys has bought an ice cream cone or a hot chocolate."

"Who buys ice cream in the winter time, Walter?"

"Well, what about the hot chocolate?"

"We only bought the hot chocolate at Clifford's because you threw us out in the cold and the snow."

"Well my god, I wish you would have told me that before I went to all this expense."

"You never asked."

Finally one cold snowy night after that explosion, Walter lined up a bunch of paper cups on the counter. Instead of pouring the hot chocolate down the drain, he poured us each a cup. He had a big smile on his face until one of the guys asked if he would put a spoon full of vanilla ice cream on top like Mr. Clifford used to do.

I snatched up my hot chocolate and ran. I knew what was coming would not be pretty.

63

Brother Conrad

Brother Conrad was the size of a midget. One of his antics was to crawl up on top of his desk at the front of the classroom and peek down on somebody who was sitting up front, maybe eating their lunch or doing something inappropriate. He would belly-flop across his desk, his head propped up by his elbows with his chin in his palms. His feet would be in the air behind him, like a little kid lying across his bed at home. Everybody in the class would go into hysterics.

No matter what class he was teaching, he always drifted over into Lawrence, its politics or people. He was very concerned about the canals. He felt they were dysfunctional and useless. He wanted them to be drained and paved or used for a subway or something.

He was brutally sarcastic. I'll never forget the day he walked into the classroom holding a copy of the Eagle Tribune high over his head.

"Lookie, lookie, lookie," he squealed. "Did you see last night's paper? We got two more."

The front page of the Tribune had a picture of a car wrapped around a telephone pole. The car was estimated to have been traveling at over 100 miles per hour. Two teenagers had been killed instantly. The vehicle was hardly recognizable as an auto.

Brother Conrad thought teenagers were violent and suicidal. He proposed a solution. He often suggested all teenagers should be shuttled off to an island somewhere. Periodically a boat could be sent to the island and extract all of those who managed to survive to the age of 21 and return them to civilization.

In World History class he had one routine that went on and on. There was a student in the class by the name of Harcourt.

"Harcourt, would you please stand up."

Harcourt (not his real name) was probably eating his lunch, looking out the window or grab-assing with someone around him.

"Tell me Mr. Harcourt, what do you intend to be when you grow up?"

"I'm goin' to be an engineer, Bruddah"

"Really? I don't really think so, Harcourt. Engineers have to know a lot of math. Are you good at math, Harcourt?"

"Not very, Bruddah. But why do you have to know a lot of math to drive a train? All you have to do is follow the tracks."

"Oh, you want to be that kind of an engineer. And you have the boots for it don't you?"

"Yes Bruddah, I got these engineer boots for Christmas."

"How nice. And you feel you can drive a train by just following the tracks. I suppose that is how you get to school each day. You are from up the river aren't you?"

"I live in Haverhill, Bruddah. But I don't follow the railroad tracks to get to school. I take the bus."

"Well, since you ride on a bus everyday to get to school, why don't you want to become a bus driver?"

"Bus drivers don't have no tracks to follow, Bruddah. I figure driving a train should be easier and I think it pays more money."

"Harcourt, you must know by now that you are never going to graduate from this school or go to college. Here it is only January. Do you realize that if you quit school right now and beat the June rush, you could get in line ahead of all the other kids over at the mill employment office and maybe get a job?"

"I want to drive a train. I don't want to work at a mill."

"Okay, okay, quit now and get your fanny down to a train station. If you wait until June, there will probably be a whole bunch of your fellow classmates ahead of you down at the train station. If you quit right now the line will be a lot shorter."

"I'm goin' to go to college, Bruddah."

"You are? And what college is that, may I ask?"

"Harvard."

"Harvard? That is a very good choice. Why did you pick Harvard?"

"Because there is a train from Haverhill that goes right to Harvard Square."

"Oh yes, I forgot. You like trains."

This comedy routine sometimes went on for the whole period. It depended on Harcourt's answers. If Harcourt's answers were creative enough, Brother Conrad couldn't resist asking more silly questions.

Our entire class flunked the World History exam. Brother Conrad just couldn't believe it. When he asked for an explanation, Harcourt raised his hand.

"Yes, Mr. Harcourt. You have an explanation of why this entire class flunked their World History exam?"

"I think so, Bruddah."

"Well, by all means share your insight with me because I am at a total loss."

"Well Bruddah, there wasn't one question on that exam about the canals, the Merrimack River, the water works, Lawrence, or even Mayor Buckley."

Jackie Greco – My Little Friend

When I was a young boy living at 32 Chelmsford St. Lawrence, Mass., my Uncle Joe died. After the funeral and burial and all, I went trudging up the stairs of our tenement house to "Grammy's." I knocked on the door as always and my Uncle Ray called out, "Come on in, Richie." He knew it was me – it was always me, every night.

I entered the apartment and it was dark. I could barely see anything. "We are in here," my Uncle Ray called again. I felt my way into the parlor. I expected somebody would turn on a light – but no one did. As objects and my uncle and my grandmother slowly came into focus, I asked, "Why are you guys sitting here in the dark?"

"Well Richie, when someone you love dies it is the custom to spend one evening sitting in the dark remembering all the things that person meant to you throughout your life. So we are just sitting here tonight thinking about your Uncle Joe and all the things he meant to us while he was alive."

I went to my usual spot on the floor between my grandmother and my Uncle Ray. My uncle tossed me my pillow and I spent that evening lying on their carpet in the dark thinking about all the things my Uncle Joe meant to me while he was alive. No one spoke.

I don't know if that is a good custom or a bad custom but it is always what I end up doing when a loved one dies.

Jack Greco and I were recently discussing when it was that we first met. Neither of us could remember. Jack suggested it may have been basketball at St. Rita's grammar school that drew us together. Jack remembered playing with me and others in my backyard. That would bring us back to the fourth or fifth grade in grammar school.

I think I can go back a little earlier than that. When I was a very young boy, about five or six years old, I hung around Walter's Variety Store by myself. Walter had a comic book section behind the front door. Walter would trade two of yours for one of his. I spent whole evenings sitting there reading and trying to make up my mind. Two of mine for one of Walter's was a big burden for me – the one of Walter's had to be really special. It took me hours to make up my mind.

Jackie Greco was also a comic book lover. I think we may have met there at Walter's rummaging through the comic books. He lived up the hill from Walter's on Willow St. Walter's was on the corner of Center and Willow. Jack collected Spiderman, Superman, Batman, Plastic man and others of that kind. I was a Donald Duck, Scrooge McDuck, Mickey Mouse kind of a guy. I think that could take us back to 5, 6, or 7 years of age.

Jack was only slightly older than me, but yet he was two grades ahead of me in school – obviously he was smarter. But I was better at playing basketball. When he was still putzing around on the low level Pintos while in the eighth grade, I was "starting" on the prestigious "Mustangs" while only in the seventh grade.

Jack would fish anywhere. I never fished but somehow we became fishing buddies. Jack would bring his pole and we would go walking along the Spicket River, in Lawrence or Methuen, in various locations – sometimes behind the Rats (Star Theater – Rats is Star spelled backwards) on Broadway and other times behind the old folks home further up on Broadway. I remember Jack even fishing in the polluted canals behind the mills down on Canal St. If he caught anything, I wouldn't let him throw it back. My mother loved fish and would eat anything. I would bring her home "hornpout" Jackie caught in the canals. My mother would clean them, bread them and pan fry them. She would sit at our tiny kitchen table smacking her lips trying to lure me into taking a bite. No way!

As we got older, Jackie got a pickup truck and a rowboat. He would fish and I would row. When he found a hot spot, I would stop rowing and read. As he fished we discussed what I found at the time transformative. I was usually very excited and predicting catastrophe or world revolution. Jackie always assured me things were as they are and will more than likely remain that way. I could never accept it but so far he has been correct.

I hate to admit this but I used to be the official flashlight holder at Jackie's kissing game parties. I was much too shy to be kissing "strangers." I didn't even kiss close relatives for god sake. Actually, it is difficult for me to believe today that I was brave enough and social enough to actually go to the party and hold the flashlight. Jackie must have talked me into that. He must have insisted. He must have!

I would go with Jackie up to his Uncle Sarkey's chicken farm. His uncle raised chickens and sold the eggs door to door. He had an egg delivery route. I remember accompanying Jackie once or twice delivering his eggs in an old, black pickup truck— it could have been green. I didn't do anything; I just sat there and kept it interesting.

I also shinned the flashlight on rats in Uncle Sarkey's chicken coops while Jackie picked them off with his 22 rifle. I think he had a pistol of some kind he used also. I must have been into flashlights in those days.

Jack fixed me up on my first official date. I guess it was called a blind date because the girl didn't know me and I

69

didn't know her. I think Jackie was worried I spent too much time reading books and not living life. Jackie is the only boy I knew who actually had girls as "friends" – not girlfriends but friends. I was amazed. What did he talk to them about? I didn't get it. He fixed me up with one of his girl "friends."

We went to the young lady's home. I walked up to the door. Her father met me. We sat down at the kitchen table. He was a widower and raising this girl on his own. He was very nervous – but he was the rock of Gibraltar next to me. He liked me. In retrospect I think he liked me a good deal more than his daughter did. When we left their little cottage, I remember looking back and seeing dad standing there with a smile on his face. I was tripping over the red brick pathway and stuttering something terrible. I'm sure after our "interview" the old man figured that if anyone was going to be taken advantage of this evening, it certainly wouldn't be his daughter. That was a safe bet.

I remember that evening as one of the most embarrassing and disappointing experiences of my young adult life. Jackie assured me that from his point of view it all worked out advantageously. The advantageous part must have come after me and my blind date were dropped off at our respective houses.

As a young teenager Jack had a bout with a very serious disease. He wasn't expected to survive. In response to this dire circumstance Jack hosted his own "going away" party. Being good old mill town, back-alley Lawrence, even that party ended up in a fist fight between two of our local moron buddies. I will withhold their names to protect the stupid.

As we all matured and got to the falling in love age – Jackie fell in love and I wrote poems to his prospective girl friends. I don't remember any of the poems. I have a very strong feeling they weren't very good. But I do remember writing them.

Jackie was a "gun" man. He liked westerns and cowboys. He had a real cowboy gun and holster. He would go up to the rod and gun club by himself and practice his quick drawing technique just like Hopalong Cassidy or whoever. On one occasion he got his quick draw technique backwards. Instead of quick-drawing his pistol and then firing, he fired and then drew his pistol. Unfortunately he shot himself in the leg. Even more unfortunate, as he hobbled around the neighborhood trying to get somebody to call an ambulance, people kept closing their curtains and locking their doors. I imagine it wasn't every day a young teenager appeared on a person's doorstep dressed like Gene Autry with a loaded pistol on his hip, wounded and drenched in blood. He got himself to a hospital somehow and lived – lucky for his future wife and two daughters.

When Jackie had to drive to Rowley, Mass to identify the body of his older sister who was killed in a tragic motorcycle accident, he called me. The undertaker and I propped him up on each side as his knees buckled at the sight. It was a long, quiet drive both ways.

When we got to college, me, Jackie and Gussie Royle drove up to the Merrimack College Library almost every evening. While I searched the archives down in the basement library for the "truth," Gussie Royle and his pals devised methods for cheating, and Jackie hung out in the lounge and the coffee shop adding names to his little black book of prospective girlfriends. I never saw either of them open a book. It always amazed me, those two jokers both graduated from college and received degrees and I never even finished.

When Jackie finally found the girl of his dreams and married, he asked me to be his best man. At the time I remember feeling I hardly qualified as a best man at anything – but he asked me, so I did it. Neither of us passed out. And neither of us got to kiss the bride as I remember. I think Jackie even asked the priest if he shouldn't kiss the bride and the priest said, "That's not necessary. You will both have plenty of time for that sort of thing." Ah yes, the good old days. I hope that memory was from the practice secession and not at the actual wedding. I can't be sure.

I have always told my wife that Jackie was one of the few guys I knew who actually "wanted" to get married. Many of my other buddies had to be "persuaded," but Jackie was damn the torpedoes, full speed ahead. He was a man with a plan, I always thought.

I think I was he and Diana's first dinner guest at their first apartment. If I am not mistaken she made Lasagna. I may have been first because she felt she needed somebody to practice on. What is it with girls and Lasagna? That's what my wife made the first time she entertained me at her apartment. Diana was luckier than my wife Carol. I went home after eating at Diana's. Carol got stuck with me for the rest of her life.

Today my little friend, Jackie, is gone. He died while I was working on this project. He had the comfort of his wife and two daughters at his bedside. Of course, I won't be forgetting Jackie and neither will any of the old gang from the corner or the Howard Associates or the Howard Ass as Ray Dolan dubbed the group. Jack was a "smiley face." He was always a happy guy and always positive. I know one thing, wherever he's at, there will be fishing.

MY LITTLE FRIEND

When I was little, I had a friend.
We said we would be friends,
... until the end.
We didn't lie.
And when he died,
... I cried and I cried
... and I cried.

McGovern's and the Den

McGovern's and the Den were on route 114 heading out by the Den Rock Drive-in Theater. As typical insane teenagers from the 50's we used to drag race out in front of McGovern's.

My friends got me into a drag race one night. I had the use of my sister's '55 Mercury. It was really a neat car and it had a stick shift. My friends were all pumped up. I pulled out in front in first gear but when I shifted into second everybody in my 55 Merc let out with a huge groan. I didn't know how to speed-shift. The other guy, with his Olds 88 hydromatic, zoomed past me like I was standing still. That experience ended my drag racing career.

I also remember playing tackle football out in the middle of the highway. That was nuts. But in those days at 9 o'clock in the evening on a Saturday night, route 114 was deserted. That also explains the drag racing – after all in order to drag race, both sides of the highway had to be used. Of course, this still doesn't explain playing tackle football on the asphalt pavement.

Both McGovern's and the Den were packed on weekends and especially after football games. Cars would circle through the Den parking lot over and over trying to nab a prime spot. Girls would cluster on the hoods of cars, giggling and laughing and attracting the boys' attention as they drove round and round.

My biggest memory from the Den was a rather interesting experience. The whole episode started on the Hampton Beach Casino boardwalk. I had a 1946 fluid drive DeSoto. It was my first car. I bought it for ten bucks. It was a Sunday evening and everybody was heading home. Four or five local girls were dashing up and down the Casino promenade looking for a ride to the Den. This wasn't so unusual. Boys and girls would often ride to the beach with one group then bum a ride home with another.

One of my buddies knew one of the girls. She was somebody's sister. We agreed to give them a lift. They piled into the backseat and me and my two buddies rode in the front seat. They each had a beach bag of clothes and we threw those in the trunk.

My old DeSoto was big. It could hold a lot of bodies. The space between the back of the front seat and the backseat was as big as in a hearse.

My recollection of our ride to the Den was quite rowdy. I was rather shy and not used to having a carload of females. They were giggling, singing songs and asking any number of silly questions. They were all quite attractive and very bold. They would ask me some provocative question and when I would stutter or the backs of my ears would turn red, they would go into a spasm of giggles.

When we got to the Den and got their bags out of the trunk, the girls all asked if they could use my vehicle to spruce up a bit before stepping out into the "lime light" of the Den parking lot. The Den parking lot was also a kind of showplace for the girls. They had to look their best. They were fresh off the beach when we loaded them up – no lipstick, no nothing.

The girls blocked all the windows by hanging up skirts and blouses and beach towels. When they finally emerged they looked like the McGuire Sisters. For you younger folks that means they looked good.

The next morning I was aroused from a sound sleep by the screaming and ranting of my outraged mother. She was running in and out of my bedroom waving pink, green and yellow panties.

It seems she had passed by my car in the backyard on her way to the garbage shed when she detected the smell of perfume and girly powder wafting from my 1946 DeSoto. She began foraging around inside the car and found several pairs of girl panties in my glove compartment.

Though my mother was quite beside herself, I was somewhat proud that my mother would think I was teenage boy enough to gather up a glove compartment full of panties.

Why the girls left their panties in my glove compartment is still a mystery to me.

Guinevere

One of the old corner gang was a very promiscuous sort – actually there were several of the same sort in the old gang. For the lack of an imaginative fictitious name, let's just call this old gang member, Joe.

Joe was a "fun little girl" finder – of course Joe was also "little." We were all little – at least for a time.

Joe was a generous fellow also. He believed in sharing.

Joe and his over active fun girl finder found this cute, blond girl from Methuen one day. From his own experience he found her to be lots of "fun." So he introduced her to the whole gang. They had their first club meeting in her bedroom at her parent's house. Where her parents were and what they were occupied with in place of their little girl, is still a mystery to all of us.

Let's call this little girl Guinevere. Guinevere was very accommodating but had one tiny hang up – as the gang has told me. Of course, I have no actual knowledge of any of this. I was busy studying my Latin responses for Father Arcanada and the Sunday Mass ceremony.

Guinevere was under the impression that sex was "dirty." This was a common notion back in the "good old days." In order to clean this whole sex business up a bit, Guinevere would never allow herself to participate in such endeavors totally naked. She would not take her socks off.

She would save sock-less love for her one true and forever love.

The boys too liked this idea and they too participated with their socks on – saving themselves similarly. Hey, sounds reasonable to me. This was "clean" sex, not safe sex. But clean sex was very important – better to save your soul by having clean sex than to have safe sex and go to hell anyway. This was a Roman Catholic thing, I think. As I understand it Guinevere had "clean" sex with every little boy in a 40 mile radius of her bedroom.

Okay, now we have the prologue to this kiddy tale from *The Decameron*.

Time passes and there we all are sitting on the steps at Nell's Variety, when down the hill from the Howard comes old Ralphie (false name – designed to protect the stupid). It is late. Nell's is closed and the streetlight has been on for hours.

"Hey Ralphie, what are you doing out so late. This is past your bedtime, ain't it?"

"Oh man, you guys are not going to believe it. I just made love up the old Howard with the future Mrs. Ralphie."

Ralphie was the kind of guy who was in love with every little girl who smiled at him. But Ralphie had a strong moral character. Although he was rather free with his sexual favors, as were most of the boys, he never had sex with a girl he wasn't intending to marry. I think this was Ralphie's version of Guinevere's sock thing. And all of his future wives were just wonderful, sweet, little homemakers.

"This girl is just terrific."

"Of course she is."

"No not because of that. She is just wonderful all over. Do you know what she likes to do most of all?"

"No what?"

"She likes to knit."

"Really, well I hope she knows how to knit baby booties."

"She likes to sew, too."

"That's great, Ralphie, tell us more."

"She bakes cookies every weekend."

"Have you eaten any?"

"No but I'm sure they are good."

"Yeah right."

"She loves kids too."

"Well, that is a good thing. It sounds like she may be having one or two … or three or four … or …"

"Oh come on! Get off it. I'm serious."

"Ralphie, you are always serious, right up until the next potential little homemaker comes along."

"Yeah but this is different. This is the real thing. I am truly in love with this girl and she is seriously in love with me. She told me I was the boy of her dreams. She said she had been waiting for me all her life."

"She has been waiting for a fat, potentially bald, sweaty little meatball like you all her life? Man, tell her to get a real life."

"I'm going to buy her a ring."

"You got enough money for the Cracker Jacks?"

"You guys are so damn funny. You all just wait and see. Guinevere is the girl for me, man."

"Did you say Guinevere?"

"Yeah."

"Well, Ralphie you may have stumbled onto the girl of a lot of guy's dreams."

"What do you mean?"

"Ralphie, everybody knows Guinevere – and most guys know her as well as you do."

"I don't care. I'm still marring her. I love her and she loves me. This is the real thing. This ain't puppy love. I mean we just made naked, passionate love up the Howard."

79

"You said naked?"

"Yeah."

"Was she naked?"

"Yeah."

"Totally naked?"

"Well ..."

"Well what?"

"Well, all except for her socks. She said she was a little cold."

"Ah huh. Well, Ralphie I wouldn't be counting your knitted baby booties before they hatch."

"What do you mean?"

"You'll find out."

As it turned out Ralphie did marry Guinevere. Such girls were loved by everybody in the good old days but yet frowned on as potential brides and mothers for some reason. It was one of those 50's or 60's things, I guess.

But in reflection and knowing the results of all the gang and the various girls of their dreams, Ralphie did about as well as most everybody else. I think he is still married to that same girl and his children are all grown and living free – or have been granted an early release. I wonder if she is still wearing her socks to bed each evening. That would be disappointing.

Boston Red Sox

I remember one kid in our neighborhood who stated in public that he was a New York Yankee fan. As far as I know they are still dredging the Spicket River in hopes of finding his remains. The family is seeking "closure," I've been told.

There were a few years back then when I memorized the entire Red Sox roster every year. My era included such greats as Ted Williams, Jackie Jensen, Jimmy Pearsall, Sammy White, Frank Malzone, Billy Goodman, Edie Joost, Harry Agganis and many more. I go back as far as my favorite first baseman Walter Dropo (1950) and through my greatest disappointment when Carl Yazstremshi replaced Ted Williams in left field (1961).

I attended only one Red Sox baseball game. I don't remember the exact year. My favorite uncle, Ray Essick, took me to a double header. I was beside myself with excitement all that day. My big dream was, of course, to see Ted Williams hit a home run. It didn't happen.

The Sox lost the first game of the double header and they were losing the second one also. It was finally the last of the ninth inning. I wanted to see any Red Sox player hit a home run, now. Each time a new player came to bat, I would start pulling on my uncle's sleeve. "Can this guy hit a home run Uncle Ray?"

"Oh yes," he would say. "That's Jackie Jensen up there. He is one of the best players ever in baseball."

We went through all the top players. They were all "one of the best ever" according to my uncle. None of them hit a home run but they did manage to load up the bases. There were two outs. They were down by three. This could be it.

"Who's up now, Uncle Ray? Can he hit a home run?"

My uncle didn't know the batter. He was a pinch hitter. He looked up the guy's number on his program. The man was listed as the third string catcher. His name was Pete Daley. My uncle shook his head in discouragement. When everybody found out who the man was at the plate the crowd groaned in disappointment.

"Well, can he? Can he hit a home run Uncle Ray?"

My uncle always tried to put a positive spin on everything, but in this case his doubt was rather obvious.

"Well, they are all professionals. A person can't play in the major leagues if he can't hit a home run. Pete Daley is kind of old. He has been around for a long time though. He's the third string catcher."

Oh man, I thought to myself, what a cop-out. "He's the third string catcher? Don't they have a second string catcher who might be better and younger?"

My uncle just shrugged his shoulders.

Pete Daley, the old, third string catcher, seemed to be just standing there letting pitches go by. Finally it was a full count. The whole game and my one double header were down to one pitch.

CRACK! Everybody leaped out of their seats. I couldn't see a thing but a sea of heads and shoulders bouncing up and down in front of me. I kept tugging at my uncle's sleeve. "What happened? What happened? Is it a hit?"

It was a grand slam home run.

My only baseball game ever and I saw Ted Williams strike out and Pete Daley, the third string catcher, hit a grand slam home run.

Ted Williams did get on base a couple of times and I watched the famous Ted Williams Shift take place – the whole left side of the field empty. That was amazing. He hit a couple of "high fly balls" up over first base but none of them carried off into the stratosphere. He made one of his famous no-look, over the shoulder catches off the thirty-seven foot two-inch Green Monster in left field

Jimmy Pearsall made some great catches too and restrained himself from attacking anybody in the bleachers. Jimmy had what they call today "anger management issues." He had a nervous breakdown and went to a mental institution. They made a movie of his life in 1956, *Fear Strikes Out*. I remember watching something on TV also. I think it was on Playhouse 90. I remember Jimmy being interviewed about his illness after the TV play.

People actually threw stuff down onto the field at Jimmy trying to get him to act up. He didn't on my day at Fenway Park. It was a great day. I have never forgotten. I promised myself I would always remember the hero of that day, Pete Daley – old man, and third string catcher. Wow! My uncle was right. You don't get to play in the pros if you can't hit a home run.

Dangerous Dancing

I was not born a dancer. For the majority of my early life I didn't dance. I don't dance today. But there was a period in my time when dancing came upon me. I consider it to have been a divine inspiration – or demonic possession – at the least, a genetic or evolutionary thing. It was the Age of Aquarius you will remember – numerous strange things were taking place.

One day dancing appeared in my life, full blown, with no prior training or warning like schizophrenia or multiple sclerosis. Dancing hit me like puberty strikes most kids. I still don't understand exactly what happened. Curiously enough it seemed to have some strange connection with alcohol.

Alcohol was the strange potion that turned me from the quiet, studious, shy and retiring, mild mannered Clark Kent, to the strange, talkative, flamboyant, totally outrageous superstar of the flying Wallendas.

My dancing was not simply exuberant. I was actually dangerous. I hurt people. I fell off several stages onto other people and their tables. Several of my dancing partners actually disappeared. No one has seen them to this day. It isn't that they ran away and hid, I think I actually tossed a few of them into outer space. They are probably orbiting and dodging space trash to this very day.

I blame a lot of this on the dances that came about in the 60's. I would pick out some cute little girl who looked like she snuck away from her chaperone or a local nunnery. She would be sitting in a corner in her white blouse and checkered skirt toying with her rosary beads. Her necklace would be a scapular draped alluringly over her shoulders. I would stumble over to her table destroying several other cocktail tables along the way. But curiously enough, the girl would accept my invitation. When we got to the stage we would both explode? She would suddenly become a vaudeville queen, bumping, grinding, jumping, squatting and leaping into the air. I would have nothing less than an epileptic fit. People would come running at me with spoons and tongue depressors in their hands but I would crouch and disappear safely into the dancing crowd.

I remember being at the 5 O'clock club one evening when the dancing demon descended upon me. I rushed to the stage compulsively – as one possessed. I asked a minimum of seven different girls along the way to accompany me to the stage. I don't really know if any of them showed up or not but it didn't matter. In those days everybody danced with themselves anyway. Who knew who was with whom? I would dance, leap into the air, spin around and then stare at whatever ended up in front of me. It was usually the backside of somebody. If it was the backside of some guy, I would jump and spin again until something popped up that was more pleasant to look at. Often I would go to the dance floor by myself and end up walking away with some girl who now thought I was the guy she came with. It was all very strange.

After I gained a reputation, I could just walk towards a clump of girls and they would scatter. I was a human cyclotron; I could bust a complicated molecule of solid, friendly, young ladies into a million frightened female particles all scattering randomly. I was nuclear, man.

Occasionally, as I approached a cluster, the girls would go into a football type huddle. One girl would eventually get shoved out from the center towards me and the others would all scatter and run for cover laughing, giggling and screeching. The faint of heart need not apply. Their behavior reminded me of the old childhood corner gang's reaction every time we threw Dolan into the Horseshoe Bar just off Park St. whenever we passed by.

Dancing in the 60's bordered on the possibility of becoming an Olympic event. I knew guys who danced just for the workout. It was a socially acceptable way to build up a good sweat one local body builder told me. Of course Jane Fonda and a hundred others eventually made millions selling their dancing workout books and tapes. Dancing to precipitate sweat became big business and still is today.

I don't remember sweating all that much. I considered dancing at the 5 O'clock Club and other such establishments to be more in the category of Roller Derby. Every time I spun around somebody would go over a railing. Today I imagine if 60's style dancing had a revival, mothers would be buying their kids protective dancing gear. I am sure they would have colorful headgear and pads everywhere. It would be a very big business.

I was eventually captured and taken to a clinic where I received electric shock treatment. Electric shock treatment was also big in the 60's – Ritalin had not been invented.

I broke out of the clinic when I heard the doctors whispering about a lobotomy. In the 60's one had to break out of such places. Of course, in today's world that problem has been solved. We no longer lock up people who appear to be crazy – and my god, they are so hard to distinguish. Today these people are FREE – many of them are now living in the sewer system in New York and New Jersey, I've been told.

Eventually I kicked the dancing compulsion. I discovered that by drinking two or three extra shots of tequila every hour, I could fall into a coma before the Dancing demon struck. My companions grew so accustomed to my passing out that they just left me lying wherever I happened to fall. They actually thought this was amusing.

One morning when I woke up straddling the yellow line on a divided highway wearing nothing but a pair of jockey shorts – thank god they were fresh – I decided something had to be done. My mother always warned me about that possibility of getting hit by a Hood milk truck or something and going to the Lawrence General Hospital with "embarrassing" underwear.

I knew I had a serious problem. Passing out in random locations was not a good habit to get into. But since I didn't have the ability or foresight to determine where I would pass out, I decided to hire my buddy Tom Kabildis.

I had gotten Tom a job carrying heavy sides of beef at S.H. Brennan's on Broadway so I knew he had the physical capacity. I offered him ten dollars a pick-up.

Tom proved to be an excellent bodyguard. He carried me from numerous dangerous locations to the backseat of someone's automobile or to one of our various retreats at Salisbury Beach on many of these unforeseen and unplanned occasions.

For a lousy ten bucks per pick-up, I got to live and Tom gained, I'm sure, a plethora of sanctifying graces and plenary indulgences guaranteeing him a much higher and more respected place in eternity. I am very happy and I feel a great sense of personal satisfaction that I was able to provide this opportunity to such a good and loyal friend. Everything has a reason, you know, even young drunken pre-adults passing out on the yellow lines of divided highways – I guess.

Morris Ravitch, Clarence Darrow and F. Lee Bailey

The Salisbury police busted into our little castle on Old Towne Way and threw a bunch of us into the pokey. Those of us who were the victims of this brutality on the part of the Salisbury police decided we would take this group of ruffians to court. After all, we were all mature, responsible adults at the time of our arrest and it was unanimous that these make believe, wannabe flatfoots had grossly overstepped their authority. Who did they think they were dealing with – a bunch of kids?

So what if we had a few beers and were a little rowdy, we were old enough to drink – most of us. We paid for our booze. We paid our cottage rent. We contributed to the financial success of the 5 O'clock Club, and the Normandy, and the Kon Tiki, Mac Jenney's, the Edward's Hotel and the Bowery and everywhere man! We were a positive attribute of the Salisbury economic community. We should have been treated with some respect! We weren't a bunch of punk kids sitting out on the corner no more. We were adults and should be treated accordingly. We worked for a living. We collected paychecks. We were big boys now. We had this same cottage for the last three years in a row. We didn't get thrown out. The place had not been condemned or anything like that. We decided to contest our fines and seek damages for being abused, mistreated, manhandled, harassed, and humiliated. We got a court date.

In the weeks before our day in court, we decided to solicit character witnesses from our beach neighborhood on Old Towne Way. Most of the neighbors agreed we had not caused a disturbance on the night in question. Of course, many of them were guys we knew who were also from Lawrence or Lowell or Haverhill and had rented their own cottage. Nevertheless a number of them agreed to come and testify on our behalf.

This was all well and good but we needed a "credible" witness. There was good old George and his family who lived across the way and a few doors down. He was a nice guy. We had him and his wife over to our place many times for a beer and some pizza or an Italian Hogie from Lena's or Tony's (Pappalardo's) Subs. He was not only a real person but also a retired cop from Haverhill. We decided to go over and talk to him about our situation.

When we told him we had been arrested for disturbing the peace he was shocked. He was right there in his cottage that night and he never heard a thing.

"Would you come to court and testify for us, George?"

"You are darn right I will! These guys down here aren't even real police. They're a bunch of part-time bozos who want to be important. I don't know how they get off arresting you guys."

"All right, George!"

When our day in court finally arrived, we gathered up all our buddies and went and got George. As we wandered, nervously around the courthouse, who do we bump into? Why, none other than the most famous barrister in all of Lawrence, Morris Ravitch.

When Morris found out that we were defending ourselves in this endeavor. He shook his head sadly and said, "That could be a big mistake, boys. You know the old saying; A man who is his own defense often ends up with a fool for his attorney. If I were you guys, I wouldn't go in there without a lawyer."

"Yeah, but we can't afford no lawyer."

"What the heck are you talking about? How many accused do we have here?"

"There's six of us."

"Okay, you got ten bucks each?" We all began shuffling through our billfolds and we each gave Morris ten bucks.

"Okay boys, you're all set. I'll see you in court."

"Don't you need to know about our case?"

"Oh yeah, what happened to you guys anyway?"

We told Morris our whole story and introduced him to George and all the rest of our witnesses.

The Salisbury cops gave their side of the story first: We were loud and noisy. All the neighbors had been calling. We were all drunks. We were out in the middle of the street waving beer bottles around. We were sitting on top of cars. We were yelling and screaming and using abusive language. We had the radio blaring. There were half naked, underage girls everywhere, and yeahti, yeahti, yeahti – the same old same old we had heard a million times.

We were all dressed in our Sunday best. One by one we told the judge of the physical and psychological abuse that had scarred our personalities – probably for the rest of our lives. We showed the judge the marks still on our wrists from the handcuffs. We contested the drunken issue. And why shouldn't girls be half naked? This was Salisbury Beach for god's sake. Everybody is half naked at the beach. If any of the girls were under age they weren't under by much and they had never mentioned it to any of us. Yes we may have been sitting on cars but they were our cars, parked in our parking spaces. But we took a special exception to the noise accusation. At this point Morris started calling the neighbors to testify.

The judge didn't seem to be buying a word of it until Morris brought up old George, the retired Haverhill policeman. The Judge even knew George. Morris asked

George if he had heard the aforementioned social disturbance.

"I'll tell ya, I didn't hear a thing. These kids are all great. I live right across the street. I have even been over to their cottage. These are all good boys."

"You didn't hear a lot of screaming and yelling?"

"I didn't hear anything."

"You didn't hear anything?" Morris emphasized. "You live right across the street and you didn't hear any noise? You didn't hear the alleged loud music? You didn't hear boys and girls screaming and yelling?"

"Nothing! I didn't hear anything."

"My god, are you deaf or what?" one of the accusing cops burst from his seat."

"Well," George said. "I have been having a little trouble lately. The doctor says my right ear is completely gone but my left ear is still working at about 50 percent. I don't hear everything these days. I have to keep the TV volume up pretty high. But I'm getting by."

The judge fined each of us forty bucks apiece. We didn't get any jail time though. Thank-you Mr. Morris Ravitch, attorney at law.

She Says She's a Mop

Lawrence is, of course, the Immigrant City. In Lawrence your ethnic heritage was a thing of pride and all your friends knew what nationality you were. I never thought much about it until I settled in the South.

In the South ethnic heritage is more simply defined – you are either black or you are white; you are a Yankee or you are a good old boy (Redneck). I have managed to pass for white here in the South but I have never gotten past being a Yankee. The minute I open my mouth some guy who looks like Baby Huey and has a whole pack of cigarettes in his mouth that he is attempting to eat but can't seem to swallow says, "You ain't from around here, are ya?"

In the South they are not much on diversity. They are all "American."

I told somebody who came to my little ice cream parlor I was part English. The rumor went around town some "foreigner" from Britain owned the ice cream parlor in Carrabelle. British tourists would come into my shop and ask me where in England I was raised. Many locals in this neighborhood think New England is a country in Europe. It is mixed in somewhere among those other countries like Ireland, Scotland, Wales, Spain, France and New England. I told one guy that Massachusetts was in New England. He said, "No way man, Massachusetts is right here on the east coast of the United States." I decided not to pursue any further debate on the issue.

But in Lawrence a person's ethnic heritage was something to take pride in. When some old, gray haired woman stuck her head out of a second story window and began chattering in gibberish, it was no big deal. From my point of view all grandmothers spoke some sort of gobblygook. It didn't bother me or any of my buddies.

Mr. Reardon, who lived next store, was Scottish. Mr. Reardon spoke English, his wife said, but whatever he was speaking was Greek to me.

He would pick me up on his way to church in his 1934 Chevy four door sedan, with the red, spoke tire rims. He would mumble something and they would both turn and look at me sitting there in the backseat of their car. After a few moments of awkward silence, his wife would say, "He wants to know how you are doing in school." It would continue like this all the way from Chelmsford St. to the Immaculate Conception Church. He would mumble. She would look at my bewildered face and then translate and I would answer.

My grandmother spoke no English that I remember. Her usual greeting was, "You workie, Richie?" As long as I "workie" she would give me a smile.

I would sit in her living room as a little boy hour after hour listening to a Polish radio station playing Polish polkas. Every half hour or so, the guy on the radio would say something in English. It went like this, "Pierogui goumphki mushtuski Haffner's gas station." Or in the middle of a long line of gibberish the announcer would throw in a Breen's funeral home or an Essem hot dogs. I thought it was all some kind of comedy show, like Sid Caesar's Show of Shows. I would laugh and Grammy would laugh because I had laughed and we both had a great time.

One day we had a minor calamity at 32 Chelmsford St. My uncle Clayton and my aunt Amelia were moving out of

93

the apartment upstairs. They were buying their own home over on Exchange St. across the street from the Polish Bakery. A new family was moving in. Our little tenement was a buzz with rumors. What would this new family of strangers be like? My mother was snooping around for information. She couldn't get much out of my uncle. She saw my grandmother sitting out on the front porch. She decided to go out and grill her. My mother spoke Polish. I could hear them jabbering. It was summer time and the windows were up with the screens in place.

They were talking for some time when suddenly my mother burst into laughter. She came running down the corridor and into the house. She couldn't stop laughing.

"What's so funny," I asked.

"The new lady upstairs, she's a mop."

"She's a mop?"

"Grammy was talking to the new lady and Grammy asked the lady what nationality she was. Grammy said the lady told her she was a mop. Grammy shrugged her shoulders and asked me if I knew what country mops came from? I couldn't figure it. I asked Grammy if she knew the lady's last name. The lady's name is Ciardello."

"She ain't a mop. She's a wop."

"Yes, Mrs. Ciardello told Grammy she was a wop and Grammy never heard of the word wop, so she figured she meant mop. So Grammy thinks Mrs. Ciardello is a mop."

"So did you straighten her out?"

"I tried. I told her Mrs. Ciardello was a wop and not a mop. But Grammy said she knew of no country called Wop or Mop. I tried to explain to her that people who come from Italy are called wops but Grammy said, wops, mops it doesn't matter to her as long as the lady pays her rent she can be a mop or a wop or whatever she wants to be."

Mabel, Violet, Bill and Harold

Jack Sheehy, Frank Duchnowski and me were VIPs at the 5 O'clock Club. We had our reserved seats at the back bar directly behind the cash register. It actually seems like we spent an entire lifetime sitting there. In truth, I suppose it was only ten or twelve years – and then only the summers. It was kinda the old Nell's how-to-start-a-corner-gang theory, I suppose. Sit and hang out and "they shall come." If it was summertime and anybody was looking for any of us, they knew where to go. We were a part of the art deco. We were the gang from "Happy Days" maturing and drinking competitively.

One of the challenges of our sentry positions behind the cash register at the back bar at the Five was to sit there each evening drinking continuously from 5 or 6 p.m. to closing at 1 a.m., and then rising from our stools and walking to the front door as if we were sober. That involved a number of pretenses – no stumbling, no stuttering, no unreasonable laughing, no knocking over chairs or tables, and saying goodnight to Mabel, Violet and Harold on the way out without slurring. Bill was usually with us each night at the bar so we already said goodnight to him. I guess we were kinda like the Walton's of the Five – goodnight John-Boy.

Mabel, Violet, Bill and Harold were the owner family who ran the 5 O'clock Club at Salisbury Beach. They were a wonderful bunch and we had a great time teasing them. Over the years we became friends. I even delivered chickens to their mother's place out on Seabrook Beach. I owned a little meat market in Lawrence and she said she loved "my" chickens. I tried to explain to her that they weren't really "my" chickens and I just bought them from John the Chicken Man at S.H. Brennan's. But she wouldn't buy that simple explanation. She felt I had put my touch onto these chickens and they were special. After awhile she actually had me wondering. Maybe it was me? Maybe I had the Midas "Chicken" Touch. It could happen, I suppose!

Harold was the Commander and Chief. Bill was an enlisted Air Force man who had married Mabel. Mabel was a challenge; she was very serious. Violet, on the other hand, could have been named Marilyn or Niki. She was very giggly and silly. One could stare at Mabel and get nothing but a curious glance in return. Violet could not take the pressure. If you looked at her, she laughed. Bill was one of the guys. He laughed, joked and teased. He caught on to our routines instantly.

Violet, Mabel and Bill were always buying us free drinks. Harold on the other hand was a hard butt. He considered himself to be a reasonable and practical man. He was an officer in the Military and a West Point graduate – and I think he actually served in the military of the United States of America after graduation as opposed to the French Foreign Legion or something like that. On top of that he was a lawyer. He didn't practice though. He was too busy tending bar, checking IDs and watering down our drinks at the Five.

Violet and Bill were the best pourers – heavy on the booze and light on the "filler." Harold, on the other hand, had to be watched closely and coached constantly.

"Harold, Harold! You were a little quick on the gin. You want to try that again and this time, I'll count to three for you."

Harold did have occasion to use his legal expertise though. He told us of one interesting case that he said set a precedent in the Seabrook annals of jurisprudence.

Now I may have this a little upside down so don't sue me Harold, but this is the way I remember it.

Harold who was no spring chicken at the time – maybe in his mid-thirties had, at long last, met the girl of his dreams and fallen in love. Harold asked the young lady for her hand. She accepted and Harold went shopping for a ring. He bought his girlfriend a lovely and very expensive engagement ring. She accepted it and promised to be his bride.

But Harold was of a very suspicious nature. He didn't get to be single in his mid-thirties by just "jumping" into things. He had been hearing rumors. He was going to hire a detective to follow her around but then decided that he should do it himself. The fact that it was cheaper to do the tailing himself was really not the issue – he explained. This involved honor, not money.

Dutchy criticized Harold's approach to the matter. "If you don't trust somebody, you shouldn't marry them," Dutch advised.

Harold smirked, indicating Dutchy's naiveté.

In the weeks and months that followed, Harold deployed many disguises and aliases culminating at a second floor bedroom window expose'. It seems Harold was so shocked at what he saw he nearly fell off his ladder. His promised bride to be was making mad passionate love to another of Harold's old girlfriends. Now even as I write this tale I become dubious of my memory but this was Seabrook, a community much ahead of the times.

Harold was so distraught over this discovery that he sued his prospective bride for breech of promise. He wanted his expensive ring returned. Dutchy contended that this was not the action of a compassionate man. He told Harold that the ring was a gift to Harold's chosen bride, someone he once loved, and it should be forgotten. Harold's eyebrows rose and his nose elevated. "Really," he said. "And this is what you would do if you were in my situation?"

"Of course," Dutchy replied. "A gift is a gift. You made a mistake and now you should be man enough to accept the consequences."

"Well," Harold said, "returning to the world of reality and the LAW. I took her to court, won my case, and got my ring returned. You see LEGALLY the ring was not a "gift." It was a contract. The ring was given on the condition of the acceptance of marriage. She failed to meet the understood conditions of the proposal and therefore she was required to return the ring."

"Yeah but she didn't say she wouldn't marry you," Jack interjected.

"Yeah, but I ain't going to marry her when she's sleeping with my ex-girlfriend for god's sake."

"So then YOU broke the contract and she should get to keep the ring," Dutch expounded.

"No, no, no, no. You can't be engaged to somebody and go sleeping around with other people."

"Really, did you guys know that?" Ducthy asked.

"Well, all I know is Nancy Mahoney got caught screwing her best man after the wedding in his car out in the parking lot behind St. Patrick's Church and she didn't give back her engagement ring or her wedding ring," Jack said.

"Yeah but the guy Nancy Mahoney married was Freddy Grogan and he got caught with Nancy's bride's maid in the lady's room. He couldn't really ask for his ring back after that."

"Not only that, Freddy borrowed the money for the ring from Nancy in the first place. So whose ring was it really?" Jack added.

"Oh my god," said Harold. "You can't talk to you guys from Lawrence about anything serious. You guys live in another world down there."

"Oh yeah? ... And Salisbury and Seabrook are in the real world, I suppose," offered Jack.

"I'll tell you what, I'm going to give you all a round on the house and let's just change the subject."

"Okay, start pouring and I'll count to three the correct way – one a thousand, ahh ... two a thousand, and ahhh ... Dutch are you timing this with your watch?" Jack asked.

"I left my watch at home," Dutch confessed sadly.

"Three," said Harold, "and that's it."

You see, one had to be good to work a free drink out of Harold.

Nell's Variety Store

Nell's was one of our corner hang outs. It was a little variety store on the corners of Center and Exchange Streets in North Lawrence. Before it was Nell's it was Contarino's. I know because they had a pretty little daughter named Anita. We migrated between Nell's and Walter's which was on Center and Willow Streets.

Nell's was owned by the Shaheen family. One of their children, Peter, went to school with most of us. George was the dad and Emily was the mom.

It wasn't until I was an adult and working for a buddy of George, Eddie Solomon, that I found out what a problem our little gang was to poor George and his family business.

Eddie Solomon had a mid-sized grocery store on Broadway. George used to stop in for a little afternoon libation a few times each week. I was a butcher and meat cutter and I was helping Eddie part-time at his store.

I was really pretty shocked to find out George's side of the story. Most of us kids thought we were an asset to Nell's Variety. After all, didn't we run to the store to buy bread and milk for mom? Didn't we contribute to their business buying soda, potato chips, candy bars and the like? Why there were at least 20 to 30 of us guys who hung out at that store on different occasions. We had to provide their little store with a lot of revenue, right?

Well, not really. It seems we frightened more customers away than what we were worth. Many of George's friends and relatives were afraid to stop at his store. Ten to twenty kids hanging around the outside of the store was intimidating to most folks. Even the folks who lived in the neighborhood would head to the opposite corner rather than pass through our ranks.

We would be flipping coins up against the wall, or sprawled all over the sidewalk playing poker or forty-fives. We'd sit on people's steps and even warm up in a tenement hallway on cold winter afternoons. We didn't think anything about it. We had done it most of our lives. Of course we never hung out in front of our own tenement houses. Our parents wouldn't tolerate it. You would think that would have given us a little message. But no, it never even entered our minds. And when people in the neighborhood yelled at us or told us to go home, we just ignored them. Our attitude was that they were just grumpy.

George and Emily even moved their store to try to escape us. He rented a store up on the next corner. It was on Lawrence and Exchange Streets across from the Howard playground. When we all came down to the old corner and everything was closed up, we couldn't figure it. Almost immediately we wandered up to Lawrence Street and started to hang out up there.

As usual the cops arrived on the scene. They always tried to break us up or chase us off. But we were accustomed to that. The cops were like a part of our hangin' out tradition. They didn't make a dent.

Finally instead of trying to chase us off, this one cop pulled up to the Nell's corner, got out of his cruiser and came over and spoke with a bunch of us. After a long conversation where we supplied all the negative answers to his suggestions, he said, "Why don't you guys just go across the street and hang out at the Howard playground?"

We all snickered. We had been trying to hang out at the Howard for years. The cops had thrown us out time after time. The minute any of the neighbors on Birchwood Road saw us gathering on the wall or up around the baseball dugout, they would be on the phone and the cops would be there in an instant.

"Okay, I am going to give you permission to hang out over at the Howard."

Was he kidding or what? The chief would have his butt in the office in two minutes.

"Okay," we all said with a laugh. "We need your name so when the other nine hundred cops come wandering up here, we can tell them that officer so and so gave us permission to hang out at the Howard."

He told us his name and he wrote it down on a piece of paper. I don't remember what his name was, but every time another cruiser pulled up to chase us off we would all chant in chorus, "Go see Officer Johnson. He has granted us permission to hang out at this park."

In the weeks that followed, we saw Officer Johnson many times. When the tenement dwellers and owners on Birchwood Road would call the police station, Officer Johnson would pull up in front of their home. We would watch him knock on their door and step inside their apartment. We couldn't believe it, but from that time on the Howard was our hang out and George and Nell's had a corner all to themselves. Officer Johnson even started an inter-corner volleyball tournament, and the gang from the Howard won. We even got our pictures in the Eagle Tribune!

Route 1

For a time back in the 60s Route 1 became the place to go for laughs, entertainment, and the mingling of the potentially mature of both sexes.

Route 1 was a long row of eateries and nightclubs. Clubs like the Flamingo, the Wigwam, and Lennie's on the Turnpike were broken up by restaurants like the Kowloon Chinese Restaurant, the Hilltop Steakhouse and the Ship. And in between those places were auto repair shacks, truck stops, diners, trailer parks and junkyards. Restaurants and nightclubs went in and out of business. There seemed to be a new and different hotspot opening every other month – and it was the same with the restaurants.

Jack, Dutchy and I would wander around from club to club looking for love in all the wrong places until finally we would get weary – or hungry. Most often we got hungry. Nothing peaks a man's appetite like a hundred and forty-six bottles of Black Horse Ale or three hundred gin and tonics. Consequently we would then go wandering up and down Route 1 hunting that "new dining experience." We were of a similar mind and most often our quest ended at a diner or some greasy spoon type joint. But every now and then we would flip out – mostly at Dutchy's instigation. He was always searching for that unusual dining experience or that unforgettable once in a lifetime happening. He would leave no rock unturned, no door closed, and no passing female untormented.

At this point in our evening we had tormented enough females to call it a weekend and we – or should I say, Dutch – was into meeting the most exotic "food" dish of his life. He wanted to go "upscale." He was tired of all the diner type waiting staffs and the gum-chewing, plastic bracelet waitresses. He wanted to go where the "rich" people go.

Jack was always rather indifferent to Dutchy's extravagancies. "You know," he would say. "A chicken is a damn chicken. You can have a $1.95 piece of chicken or a $14.95 piece of chicken."

One weekend we three stooges went to Chinatown in New York City. In the middle of Chinatown we went into a Chinese restaurant – of all places. Dutch and I ordered two unknown never experienced before Moo Moo Cow Pies and then came Jack.

"You got any American chicken in this joint?"

Jack had been somewhat turned off by all the un-refrigerated "Chinese" chickens dangling in the fresh air out on the sidewalks and in all the Chinese grocery store windows up and down the streets of Chinatown.

"American chicken? What you mean American chicken?" responded the frustrated Chinese waiter.

"I mean American chicken – you know raised here in America?"

"All our chicken waised in America. Eb-bee-ting here waised in America."

"Could you go to the kitchen and get an American chicken that I can look at?"

"No lookie ... you order or you get out. We American and we sell American chicken."

"Okay, okay ... don't get your chopsticks all bent out of shape. I'll have an American chicken sandwich with extra mayo, light on the lettuce, hold the tomato, and I want

104

that on American white bread, no butter. You got Wonder bread?"

"No Wonder bread. We got American white bread – no Wonder bread. You want Wonder bread get the hell out of here and go get Wonder bread."

"No Wonder bread ... can you believe this place?"

At the World's Fair, Expo, in Montreal Canada in 1967 at the restaurant inside the Japanese Pavilion John Robert Michael McSheehy Sr. ordered the Pearl Harbor Special.

"What you talkee about? Dare no Pearl Harbor Special on dis menu?"

"I know; I know ... surprise me. Give me anything that wouldn't be considered poisonous in America, okay?"

I think Jack was the original model for the movie the Ugly American. But as hard as this is to believe Jack was the John Wayne, the Quiet Man of the group. He was very Gary Cooper-like. He didn't say or do a whole lot but when he did, it was usually serious and often difficult for the average bystander to grasp fully. Of course, Dutch and I sat like mannequins. We always figured Jack spoke so infrequently that when he did, the moment should be honored. When Jack spoke ... Jack spoke – and that was it.

So there we are wandering up and down Route 1 looking for Dutch's new "dining experience." Suddenly there it was. It looked like a mirage, something out of the Arabian Nights ... or the Italian Nights or the Greek Nights. We pulled into the parking lot. It was snowing. It had been snowing lightly but now it was starting to accumulate. Jack parked his used, green, Ford Valiant with the large dent in the driver's side door and the plastic statue of St. Christopher on the dashboard, between a Lincoln Continental and a fire-engine red Corvette and we went hustling up to the ornate, Ali Baba-like entrance. This was a real fancy joint.

"The chicken in this joint is probably $18.95," Jack suggested.

We stepped inside the lobby and began stamping our feet on the royal blue carpet and dusting the snow off our Eisenhower style, wool lined windbreakers. Dutch was just about to pull off his knitted black winter cap. His mother knitted it and Dutch liked it because when it got really cold he could roll it down to cover his ears. But before he even removed his cap or wiped his runny nose, the maitre d' in his tuxedo with the frilly white, lacy cuffs sticking out of the sleeves was on top of us. He was a little guy obviously suffering from a Napoleon Complex. He rushed over to us and very aggressively grabbed onto Dutch's arm and started ushering him to the exit.

"This place is not for you gentlemen," our little friend remarked sarcastically rounding the three of us up like cattle. "There's a nice 'diner' up the road that you guys would really like a lot better – lots of baked beans and greasy fried potatoes. This way 'boys'."

Dutch was suddenly inspired by the little man in the tuxedo. Without any hesitation, he removed the man's hand from his arm and as he straightened his wool cap and wiped his runny nose on the sleeve of his jacket, announced.

"We ain't here to eat, pally. We are here to get a couch. There it is right over there – that purple one with all the roses on it. You guys are six months behind on your payments for that couch. We're here from the furniture company. They can't wait any longer."

There was a fancy couch sitting in front of the receiving desk. There was another fellow in a tuxedo taking reservations over the telephone. "Let's get it, Ralphie," Dutch instructed while looking towards me.

"Well, okay Alice," I said to Dutch. And the two of us went over and each grabbed an end of the couch.

The little tuxedo ran up to the big tuxedo and the two of them began whispering to one another. The big tuxedo began dialing his phone like a mad man. The little guy didn't know what to do.

We were half the distance to the entrance (and/or exit), with the couch in hand, when the little guy came running to Dutchy's side. "Hey guys give us a break. This is the weekend. We'll straighten it out Monday."

"Yeah, the boss said you said that last time. This time he told us not to accept any excuses. The couch is going back. You can call Monday and cry on his shoulder. But we got to get going. We've got two more stops before we can bring the truck back to the garage. The snow is already piling up. We got to get moving."

At this point what appeared to be the entire kitchen staff, complete with cutlery and other weapons came strutting menacingly into the lobby led by the large tuxedo. Dutch and I had the fancy couch almost outside the glass French style door entrance. Jack had anticipated the eventual outcome of Dutch's strategy and the get-a-way Valiant was puffing smoke a few feet away. We dropped the couch and jammed it against the doors from the street side. As the cutlery crew pushed and shoved at the blocked entrance, we hopped into the Valiant and Jack slipped and slid out of the parking area.

We decided that it would be wiser to proceed toward home and evacuate Route 1 as quickly as possible.

We stopped for chow at the Danvers Diner. We all had bacon and eggs, greasy fried potatoes and lots of Boston baked beans. Jack always put ketchup on his baked beans and Dutch liked to mix everything together like it was a stew or something. I liked everything in its own place and I got my beans on the side – no ketchup. I hate it when the beans touch the bacon or the egg yoke gets onto my greasy fried potatoes. It makes me want to gag.

And that little guy in the tux back at Abracadabra's restaurant thought we had no class. I hope we were a lesson to him – never judge a book by its cover or underestimate the ingenuity of three guys in windbreakers and one guy in his mother knitted wool cap that could be pulled down over his ears when it gets really cold.

Dr. MacShea and Miss McPheebe

Dr. MacShea and Miss McPheebe's sojourns to St. Rita's schoolhouse on the corner of Arlington and Hampshire Streets constituted the bulk of my medical care as a child. It really seems shocking to me today when I observe my nieces and nephews caring for their kids – and themselves. I would have considered my nieces and their children all to be little sissies. I learned that going to the doctor, any doctor, was a sign of weakness.

I was able to get passed Miss McPheebe and her eye charts right up until the eighth grade. I would memorize what the kids in front of me were saying. I thought of the whole event as a sort of game. It was me against Miss McPheebe. The last thing my mother needed to hear was that she had to buy another of her kids an expensive pair of glasses.

I really thought the eye chart thing was a joke. Were these other kids really seeing anything more than a big E? Some of them had to be seeing something. Certainly everybody was seeing more than I was seeing. But who cared? I had no intention of reading any dumb books anyway.

The eighth grade nun kept setting traps for me. First trick she pulled on me was to have me stand up in front of the whole class and read some scrawl she had written on the blackboard at the front of the room.

What blackboard? Was she kidding me? I always sat in the last seat in a back row. All the girls and the teacher's pets sat up front.

When she found I couldn't read any of the scribbles she wrote on the blackboard, she ordered me to sit in the first seat in the first row. Oh man was that embarrassing. All the girls in the class giggled.

Her next trick was to make me read out loud to the whole class. When she saw my face was so close to the page that I could turn the pages with my nose, she asked for my mother's telephone number. I told her we didn't have a phone. We didn't.

She gave me a note to give to my mother. I knew that one – the note went right into the sewer on the way home. Next she asked me to tell my mother that she wanted to have a talk with her. Yeah right!

When she finally asked why my mother hadn't come down to see her, I made up this story. "My mother says she pays good money here to have you people take care of things. If she has to come down here every five minutes for one thing or another she wants her money back." I made this statement in the classroom and all the other kids laughed. The nun then turned my case over to Miss McPheebe.

I considered Miss McPheebe to be like a junior warden supervising the St. Rita's Penitentiary. She gave me an individual eye test – just me. I couldn't see squat but I had the eye chart lines memorized. I rattled them off one after another. They were all wrong. Miss McPheebe had switched charts on me. What a sneak!

Miss McPheebe actually came to my house on 32 Chelmsford St. and told my mother I needed glasses.

I got the glasses but I didn't wear them. The nun forced me to stand up in front of the whole class and put them on. I was of the opinion that "real boys" didn't wear glasses.

The glasses really improved my basketball game though. That net actually had a rim holding it up. Wow!

Then came physical examination day. The girls got the day off. All us boys lined up in the corridors and stripped down to our jockey shorts. Imagine a whole school full of almost naked boys, all nervous and sweaty. This was probably the first time ever that any of us had our clothes off in front of a woman other than our mothers. If I close my eyes and concentrate, the pungent odor that permeated those hallowed corridors returns to fill my nasal passages. Its memory is almost as repugnant to me as the odor of the corned beef and boiled cabbage that filled my apartment hallway on St. Paddy's Day. Whoa, barf city! Being a combination of Polish and Irish, I was boiled-cabbaged to death.

But you know, I have always wondered how come large groups of people smell funny when they are naked and okay when they are clothed. It's weird. Next time you capture a large group of people, make them strip down and you will see what I mean.

When we got to Dr. MacShea and Miss McPheebe we had to do a number of stupid things. Like stand on one leg, touch our toes, and touch our noses with our eyes closed. Then we each had to kneel on a chair. Miss McPheebe stuck her finger in our jockey shorts waist band and instructed us to lean backwards as far as we could. When we did Dr. MacShea took a sneak peek at our ding-a-lings – Miss McPheebe got a free shot also.

When I talked to some of the other boys later, they all felt the same way. Dr. MacShea and Miss McPheebe must have been some kind of perverts. Why else would they be sneaking peeks at all our ding-a-lings? And these people were supposed to be professionals – a doctor and a nurse for god's sake. It was difficult to believe.

Today my attitude has matured somewhat. Nobody was charged for any of those health exams. I have no doubt Dr.

MacShea and Miss McPheebe received no hazardous duty pay for any of this business. Of course, in those days, the good nuns received no wages either. It seems ludicrous that my mother complained to me constantly about the cost of sending me to a "private" Catholic School. Dr. MacShea and Miss McPheebe must have been some very special people – not to mention the dedication of all those nuns. It should go without saying that I no longer think of any of them as "perverts."

Jack Sheehy

So how long have I known John Robert Michael McSheehy Sr.? Well, I suppose there were a couple of years in the beginning of my life that I didn't know Jack, but they were very few. The psychologists say that love is mutually compensating neuroses. Well in the love that constituted our life long friendship, I was certainly the neurotic and Jack did a lot of compensating. Jack was my sounding board. We talked and talked and talked. That is not exactly true. I talked and talked and talked and Jack listened and listened and listened.

My wife has been my sounding board for the last thirty years, but she has never been as good a sounding board as Jack. She talks back sometimes. Jack never talked back – most of the time he laughed. Occasionally he would say, "F'em Nobes, if they can't take a joke, just F'em." He never questioned my motives. He knew where I was coming from and he knew that was a good place to be from. He had trust in my good spirit and my intentions – if not always in my judgments and decisions.

I made him laugh. I did so many right things for the wrong reasons and so many wrong things for the right reasons, that I was funny to him. I was often more funny in his eyes than when viewed from my own perspective. When I would relate my latest tragedy to him, I would even make me laugh.

I made his mother laugh too. I can remember sitting in the Sheehy's little kitchen on Center St. As kids we used to stand out on the sidewalk and yell our buddy's name up to the proper tenement floor. We would direct the volume of the yell by cupping our hands on each side of our mouth.

"Hey Jack-eee," I'd scream. His mother would come out onto the porch and say, "Come on up, Richie."

I liked Mrs. Sheehy. I would go bounding up the stairs trying to think of what stupid kind of a story I would make up for her this week. She loved to hear me talk about my mother. She was raised with my mother in Lawrence. They knew one another as kids. Mrs. Sheehy knew what a proper lady my mother was. So when she would ask what my mother was up to these days and I would tell her that mom had just got a job driving a forklift or running the crane at the city dump or driving a sixteen wheeler cross country, Mrs. Sheehy would crack up laughing.

"It is not the smell of the garbage from the dump that bothers the rest of us in the family so much; it's those little stubby cigars she's smoking now. You know those Italian rope things? Boy do they smell."

I'd have Mrs. Sheehy rolling on the linoleum before I left. I'd still be hitting her with one-liners as Jack would be pushing me along out the front door. "Come on Groucho, let's move it."

We went to grammar school together. We went to high school together. We went to college together. We hung on the Corner together – several Corners. We thumbed to the beach together. We went to the CCHS dances together. We rented cottages at the beach together. We sat in a hallway on Park St. on many a cold winter evening next to Erslow's bakery eating Sicilian style pizza. We liked it because it was BIG and it sold for ten cents a slice. It was like good Italian sauce on a half a loaf of fresh Italian bread.

We would walk all the way over to the Immaculate Conception Church to get homemade lemon slush. There

114

was a guy on Park St. near Bassit's Hardware, Sam's, I think, who had something similar but we liked the guy over by the church. Walking didn't bother us. We walked everywhere. We had a game we played. We called it "flipping." We would walk to an intersection then stop and flip a coin – heads we go left, tails we go right. We walked all over Lawrence and Methuen.

I have been a writer forever and when I started Jack got first crack at all my poems and short stories. His criticism was always the same, "You always write exactly what happened. You are hung up on the truth. You think you have to live everything before you can write about it. If you want to be a real writer you have to forget about the truth and learn to make things up."

When Jack finally read my book *A Summer with Charlie* he said, "Nobes, I don't know what is happening to your memory but you screwed everything up in this book. The only thing that is true and really happened is Chucky was in the Navy and stayed with us one season at the beach and then he died. The rest is total fiction."

I said, "Aren't you proud of me. I finally wrote a story I made up, just like you have been telling me to do all these years." He laughed.

Me, Jack and Dutch grew into drinking companions. When we got old enough to get served and could drink "indoors" we would sit around at some club or bar after work each evening and talk all night. Well, me and Dutch would talk and Jack would listen. We did this for years. We were the three 'old maids'. All the other guys had deserted the Corner and run off and gotten married.

One evening after about eleven or twelve years, Dutch and I realized Jack never said anything. We said we have to get Jack into this talking business. Dutch and I decided we would dedicate a special evening each week to conversation initiated by Jack.

The first week we tried it. Jack said, "Screw you two guys. You guys say the same thing every night and you think you're having a new conversation. All you guys do is manipulate the letters a little and change the punctuation here and there and you think you said something new. It is the same old stuff every night – night after night after night."

Dutch and I were rather shocked. We not only thought we were having new and stimulating conversations every night, we thought Jack was having a good time too. Now the first time we let Jack speak and he hits us with this.

"Well then," I said. "How come when we call you every night – like we have been doing for the last forty years – you always come with us? We were both under the false impression that you were having a good time."

"I am having a good time."

"You are? Listening to us say the same thing over and over every damn night? How can that be fun?"

"I have fun if the people around me are having fun. As long as you two buttholes are happy, I'm happy."

"All right! Did you hear that, Dutch? Jack is happy as long as we are happy. And if we are ever NOT happy, we will just carry Jack off to a nearby table with people sitting there who appear to be happy, set him down and then he will be happy too."

"Okay, you see now," said Dutch. "You shared that with Rich and me and now we know how to make you happy. That's great Jack. You did really well on your first time out of the garage with this conversation business. Now next Thursday we are going to let you talk again. You have a whole week to think of something 'new' to say. Now don't give us this 'I'm happy if your happy stuff' next week. We want some NEW conversation. And don't try just moving the letters around because, thanks to you, we are now onto that trick."

"Oh F--- you guys," Jack said, "Can we get another round of drinks over here? These two clowns are running out of conversation and they're blaming me. They need something to jar their tongues loose and kill a few more brain cells."

Over the years, I have had the good fortune to always be able to reach Jack via the telephone at the Pizza Pub and practice my latest routine on him or relate my most recent tragedy.

One Friday evening when I needed a boost, I gave Jack a call. I had completely forgotten it was Friday night – Jack's busiest night at the Pub for call-in pizza orders. I had a few beers and was babbling away. We talked until 10 or 11 o'clock. Jack laughed and laughed and never said a word about his business. I found out later from one of the help that people were trying to call all night but every time he went over to Jack to remind him he was in the business of selling pizzas, Jack would wave him off and say, "I'm talking to my buddy Nobes, don't bother me."

When Ray Dolan, one of the old gang, died they had a reception/party of sorts, I was told. Everything was free and paid for by the Dolan family. When it was over one of Ray Dolan's kids came over to the table where Jack and the other Howard Associates were sitting. "We have a problem," Dolan's kid said. "We ran out of money before everybody got tired of drinking. We're short seven or eight hundred dollars." While the guys tried to figure out how much was in the treasury and where to find the treasurer, Jack got up from the table and went into the men's room. When he returned, he handed Ray Dolan's son the required number of hundred dollar bills. "That's from the Howard Associates," Jack told him. It seems Jack always kept a little cash money in his shoe to cover emergencies. When I was told that story, I was not the least bit surprised. It was just what I would have expected Jack to do – if he could.

He loved the town of Lawrence and its people. He wasn't going to leave even if it meant making the Pizza Pub into a military style bunker with bars on the windows and bulletproof doors. Everyplace was Lawrence to Jack – simply buildings and people with a barroom here and there.

Jack grew up to be that little Irish Leprechaun we chased around the corridors of St. Rita's grammar school as kids every St. Paddy's day. Catch that little elf and you got to share in his pot of gold. He had money for every cause and a little for anybody whenever he could – even if their cause was not all that heartbreaking or justified. He was my shamrock and good luck charm. He never stopped smiling or laughing. He was born under the astrological sign representing laughs, good times, and happy memories. He was the same for a lot of folks.

Jack died yesterday – Friday, August 14, 2009.

I know what is going to happen now. I'm going to get feeling low and my mind will say, Give your buddy Jack a call down at the Pizza Pub. By the time I get to the phone and start looking through my numbers, it will hit me that there is no more Jack and I can't call him. I'm going to be sitting at the phone holding back the tears and trying to remember how his laugh sounded.

I hope you get a good table up there Mister Sheehy – Mister John Robert Michael McSheehy Sr. – and if the other people at your table are not all that funny, give me a call. I'll think of something.

Julian's Problem

Julian was a grammar school buddy of mine. I remember riding my bike up Park St. to call Julian. With Julian on the crossbar or handlebars of my little red bicycle, we would ride over to Johnny Welsh's house to play or hang out.

Julian had no yard to play in but Johnny lived in a complex with a few tenements clustered onto a big lot. We had plenty of room for stickball, outs, or catch. We had old baseball gloves and could kill a whole afternoon just tossing a baseball around a dirt yard or hitting a few grounders.

I met Johnny and Julian in the first grade at St. Rita's. Julian had a very noticeable problem in school. It was not so noticeable in the earlier grades but it became more and more noticeable as we progressed through the grades. Julian had big trouble with oral reading. Now me and Johnny were not all that great either. We used the old finger pointing technique, going from word to word on the page and we stuttered over sounding out unfamiliar words too. But Johnny and I gradually improved. We were never great at it, but other kids didn't laugh at us when our turn came. Julian, on the other hand, got the kids giggling. He was exceptionally bad.

By the time we were all up to the fifth and sixth grade he was still reading on a first and second grade level. The fifth grade nun was a toughie. She had no sympathy for Julian. I felt bad for him but many in the class laughed. It was easy to laugh when a kid in the fifth grade was stumbling over words like 'running' and 'jumping'. Everybody figured Julian wasn't doing his homework. He wasn't practicing his oral reading at home or wherever.

I knew Julian wasn't stupid. We played together all the time. He spoke as well as anybody and he certainly wasn't dumb. Me and Johnny were both considered somewhat smart (for boys) and we were better at sports than Julian. So Julian started drifting off – even from Johnny and me. He made the grammar school basketball team but he never started (played on the 1st team) and only got to play when we were winning by a good margin.

The fifth grade nun figured Julian was just goofing off or being a wise guy. She would call on him for oral reading all the time. When the class broke up laughing she took up standing behind Julian and giving him a little slap to the back of the head every time he stuttered over a word. She would also use her "clicker" to poke him behind the ear or on the shoulder. Occasionally she poked a little too hard even for Julian who had become accustomed to her abuse. He would jump from his desk and grab the afflicted area.

When the nun finally realized Julian wasn't going to sit for her "encouragements," she resorted to a tall pointed dunce cap. She sat Julian in one of the corners in the front of the room and made him sit there with his dunce cap on his head for the entire class. By this stage most of the kids weren't laughing anymore. I know I sat in dread waiting for her to call on Julian to read. It was unpleasant to watch this day after day.

When the dunce cap petered out and Julian continued in his negative demonstrations, she ordered Julian to come to the front of the room and crawl under her desk. I can still see Julian scrunched up under her desk as the class progressed. I don't remember anything the teacher was teaching, but I do remember Julian sitting there. He never cried. He never protested. He sat there with his head hidden against his knees. I remember feeling terribly guilty and, of course, very sad for Julian. But what could be said? He should be practicing his reading. He should have been improving. He clearly wasn't trying. So under the teacher's desk or in the corner with a dunce cap on his head was the appropriate consequence.

One day while Julian was sitting under the teacher's desk a woman's face peeked through the tiny window in the classroom door. I saw the woman looking in. Suddenly the door flew open and there was Julian's mother. "Where is my son," she demanded. "I know this is his classroom, now where is he?" Julian remained under the teacher's desk. Julian's mother went directly over to the nun. The nun rose from her chair and Julian's mom boldly pushed her chair aside and looked under the desk. "Oh my God," she said. "Julian told me about this but I did not believe him. Come out from under there son." After Julian reluctantly crawled out from under the teacher's desk, his mother pulled him to her side. "What is wrong with you," she demanded staring heatedly into the teacher's eyes.

This was a difficult situation to analyze for us young tough Lawrence kids. Was Julian a sissy because he told his mother about being punished in school? Did the nun have the right attitude or was Julian's mother justified?

Julian was never considered a tough guy. He had no schoolyard reputation to uphold. He was always rather quiet and sensitive and, of course, got more so as the school years went by. Some of the nuns in the earlier years just passed Julian by when it came to oral reading or instructed him to practice more at home and never called on him again. I don't know what grades Julian got in his other subjects but he was promoted each year and was moved along. I figured he was simply a poor oral reader. Some kids were afraid to read out loud or to stand up in front of the class and recite or complete a math problem on the blackboard.

The nun and Julian's mother went out into the corridor. I really don't remember what was the consequence of that day's events but many, many years later, I bumped into Julian at the 5 O'clock Club at Salisbury beach. I remember being excited to see Julian again after all the years. We had a few drinks and talked. He had grown up to be a sensitive and well spoken young man. We talked of those days back at St. Rita's. This was the first I ever heard of dyslexia. I remember thinking at the time that he was making this dyslexia thing up but it didn't matter to me. We all go through our tough times and we all grow up.

It was a week night at the beach and I was the only cottage member who was staying at the cottage full-time. We both had a number of drinks and Julian told me he was going to spend that night sleeping in his car because he didn't feel sober enough to drive back to Lawrence. I invited him down to the cottage. I told him no one was there but me and we had a number of empty beds. He accepted my invitation and slept over that evening. We went out to breakfast in the morning and I remember thinking what a nice kindhearted person little under-the-teacher's-desk Julian had grown up to be.

It was only two or three weeks later I met Julian at the 5 O'clock Club once again. We were both in the same condition as the first meeting and I invited him back to the cottage. He refused. Accepting once was fine but he couldn't impose every weekend. I insisted but he declined.

I read in the paper that next morning that Julian R, a young male from Lawrence, Mass, was found dead in his automobile with the engine running. His car was parked in a public parking space at the end of the beach.

I couldn't believe it. I had told him he could come over to our place any week night. The place was empty for god's sake. But he couldn't impose. He didn't want to be a "sponge" or a "leach." It was so senseless and I felt so bad. Why?

I have always had the same problem with death. I find all death a tragedy. I agree with Ernest Hemingway who considered every life a tragedy, because every life ends in death. I can't make qualifications either. I can't say well he was a bad guy, or he drank too much, or he deserved to die because he didn't live properly, or he was old. I do understand there are some people who are better off being put to sleep for the sake of the rest of us, Adolf Hitler and Osama bin Laden for example, but nevertheless I find nothing that excuses the tragedy of death. I find the whole thing totally unjustified from any point of view. It is always sad. I have learned very little from my many experiences watching it happen to others. But as with my grade school buddy, Julian, there is absolutely nothing I can do about it. There is nothing any of us can do about it. We can only watch as our friends, relatives, brothers and sisters, cousins, aunts, uncles, wives, husbands, grandparents, boyfriends and girlfriends, treasured family pets, celebrities, national heroes and in some cases, our own children die right before our eyes. It is no fun – no fun at all.

Fazio's Beauty School

I don't know how the beauty school bubble got inflated in the 50's and 60's but it was big. In Lawrence there was Fazio's Beauty School. My mother is a past graduate of Fazio's Beauty School. This fact is really more amazing than any of you realize. My mother had serious difficulty in certain areas – reading, learning and school for example. She always claimed my father never graduated from high school but that she had. Whenever she made this claim I demanded to see her diploma. She would run off to her bedroom and start foraging in an attempt to add fire to this obvious exaggeration. She was never able to produce that high school diploma but threatened that one day it would turn up and then she would have the last laugh.

It took my mother 11 years to pass her driver's license test. My older sister gave mom driving lessons for several years, then I took over and my older brother actually gave it a try for a year or two. It had become a sort of family tradition. I anticipated my oldest son would take up the burden when he came along.

My sister's reaction to the experience was one of frustration. I became seriously frightened. I had nightmares that by some fluke of fate, my mother would actually have a good day and the guy at the driver's license bureau would pass her. It didn't happen while she was under my tutelage.

My brother was a saint. He had the best reaction of any of us. After every driving lesson, he would walk in the kitchen door, take one look and me or my sister and burst out laughing. My sister and I would both nod our heads knowingly.

But my mother did have her areas – knitting, sewing and doing hair. She was the daughter in her large family who did everyone's hair.

I had the same attitude towards Fazio's Beauty School as my mother did towards the first Kentucky Fried Chicken joint that opened up in our neighborhood. As I remember it was on Broadway on the next corner just past the Star Theater heading towards Essex St. (Daisy St.) My mother said, "Why in the world would anybody buy something as simple to cook as fried chicken from a store? That joint will be out of business in a week." And as you all know, she was right again. It moved to a bigger location leaving that corner to become a Syrian sandwich shop, specializing in homemade kibbi salad sandwiches which, of course, were served on fresh Syrian bread and topped with a fantastic secret Syrian dressing.

When all the girls, including my mother in her mid-life crisis, started signing up at Fazio's beauty school, I said, "Why would anybody go to beauty school when everybody has a sister who will do it for nothing." And, of course, I was right as usual. I also predicted the early demise of McDonald's and gave the Carol Burnett show no more than a month on the air.

Frankie Avalon actually recorded a song admonishing young girls for dropping out of high school and going to beauty school. I bet he thought he was pretty cleaver too.

One of my good buddies married a graduate of Fazio's beauty school and to this very day they have a thriving beauty business. Today they have a school teaching all the various techniques of hair and skin care.

Some of the old gang question our good buddy's importance in this enterprise. I've been told they actually got together and hired a detective agency to follow our pal around in an attempt to find out what he actually does to contribute to this company's viability. After several months of intense investigation, the agency reported that they had no idea what this fellow's actual responsibilities are – and to this day nobody really knows what the heck he does. I suppose we could ask his wife but you all know how women are. Women and their men are like guys and directions. They just go on and on. But I have confidence he is responsible for something even if no one yet has been able to determine exactly what it is.

Einstein had the very same problem at the Princeton Institute for Advanced Study. To this day no one knows what Einstein actually accomplished at Princeton. I always felt that if he wasn't such a radical and maybe if he studied a little harder he might have gotten into Harvard. As it was there were many Americans who wanted to have him deported because of his unpatriotic attitudes towards war and the draft ... $E = mc^2$ or not.

I have a niece who once worked at the Yellow Blueberry on Las Olas Boulevard in Fort Lauderdale, Florida. She made more in tips in one day coloring hair than I ever earned in a week. Of course, she had a lot of "funny" looking friends – but don't we all.

Now my mother, on the other hand, never got past doing her sisters' hair. You might be saying, Well if she never got her driver's license how could she get a job if she couldn't even drive to work?"

Well, she did get her driver's license. I could not believe it when she came walking through the kitchen door waving that license in her hand. I asked her for the name of the man who had passed her at the driver's license bureau. I went down to the office and spoke with him.

"Did you have an applicant by the name of Mary Noble recently?"

"I have had an applicant by the name of Mary Noble about once every month for the last eleven years," he said defiantly.

"Yes," I said. "And on each of those occurrences over those eleven years you have been consistently wise enough to flunk her. She returned home last week with a certified driver's license in her hand. Do you have an explanation?"

"Not a good one," he said. "Basically, I figured she was not going to quit trying and if I kept flunking her she would probably keep returning until she killed the both of us."

"So you just decided to let her loose on the general public?"

"Better them than me," he said lowering his head and returning to his paperwork.

There is of course a very important lesson to be learned from this sad story. The lesson as I see it is, What the heck is wrong with your daughter or mother going to beauty school? Or, Why should anyone take advice from Frankie Avalon?

The Ragman

Okay, everyone out there who remembers feeding the ragman's horse please raise their hand.

The ragman in my neighborhood was a brown-skinned, chubby little guy. My staff of researchers has informed me that the ragman's name in our era was George Layland. "Rumor" had it that George died a millionaire.

He had an old horse that pulled his junk wagon. He had a thin whip and at varying intervals he snapped the horse from a slow walk to an even slower walk – my kind of horse. As the ragman, rolled very slowly up and down the streets of our neighborhood, he would chant ... zharr rags, zharr rags. He would buy bags of rags and old clothes. He would also take broken bicycles, wagons, busted scooters ... anything. He never paid anybody very much for their junk. My mother complained about him all the time. But nevertheless, he filled that old wagon up every day.

When someone from one of the tenements would halt the ragman, he would tie his horse up to a telephone pole and little kids would gather all around to touch and pet the old horse. Some of us would run off hunting grass or pulling up straw-like stuff that grew around the fence edges or popped out of the cracks in the curbing. The old horse liked apple cores, carrots and bananas also.

The horse always pooped along the street somewhere. My grandmother would be off her rocker and out into the street with her snow shovel. She would tote the poop out behind the garages in the backyard and spade it into the dirt around her greens and her rhubarb. It was great fun finding a kid who had never eaten rhubarb before. We would all stare silently and wait as he took his first big bite and started chewing. When his face puckered up, the roar of laughter would erupt.

The fruit and vegetable vendor would set all the neighborhood moms scurrying also. I was told his name was McMartin. He had a truck and a hanging scale dangling at the rear of his truck. I am sure the Department of Weights and Measures never accessed that scale.

He crawled up and down the streets never getting out of first gear. He would yell out ... Apples, peaches, water mel ... loans. He would sing it. It would start off high with the apples and peaches and then trail off into the water mel ... loans. Apples ... peaches ... water mel ... loans.

When the price was right my mother would buy a bushel of something and have me cart it down to the landing in the cellar. The cellar was always the coolest spot, even in the summertime. The peaches, pears or apples on the cellar landing would last a good while and provided a nice treat. When the fruit started to overripe we had pies. That was an all around good deal.

Then we had the Hood Milk delivery truck guy, who arrived early every morning and left clanking glass bottles of milk on the doorstep. Each jug had a cup or so of cream floating at the top of the bottle.

Me, Ray Dolan and Jack Sheehy once applied for jobs at the Hood Milk Company on one of our unemployment walking tours of Lawrence. When the man asked us why we applied for a job at Hood Milk he caught us off guard. He clarified his question by mentioning that he had placed no ad in the newspaper asking for help. Our method for finding a job had nothing to do with checking want ads. We would just go wandering off each morning and walk into anyplace we figured had more than a mom, dad and junior employed there.

The man's question seemed rather stupid, I thought. Hood Milk had numerous milk trucks, hundreds, running all over town. Every milk truck had a driver. One of the drivers could have died over the weekend, maybe fell out of the damn truck or got a better job mowing the lawn in the Common or running numbers for one of the many local bookies. What kind of a question was this guy putting forward?

Jack and I sat there dumbfounded but Ray went into a prayer type monologue about all the things he loved and cherished about Hood Milk and being a delivery man. Ray loved the white milkman suit and the white police cap that topped it off. He loved the taste of Hood milk ever since he was a baby. One look at that Hood milk bottle sitting on the kitchen table with all the thick, rich cream floating near the top of the bottle and even his mother's breast was a second rate substitute. He finished his love story about the Hood Milk Company with, "Ever since I was a little boy, I always dreamed of one day becoming a milkman and delivering Hood milk door to door. If I were to get a position here today, it would be the highlight of my entire life – a dream come true."

The interviewer was quite impressed. A tiny tear came peeking out from the corner of his right eye. He pulled himself together, cleared his throat and told Ray that in his entire career he had never heard an applicant make such an emotional plea. Jack and I sat speechless.

When we got outside to the parking lot Jack and I both confessed to Ray that we had similar thoughts as children ourselves. The white uniform and the white police cap were especially vivid memories.

Ray said, "You guys got to be kidding me. I hate milk. The sight of the stuff makes me gag. I never thought of being a milkman once in my life."

"You made that whole thing up? How did you ever think of that?"

"Well, I figured here's this sucker stuck down there in the Hood milk building all his adult life. He probably started out as a milk delivery man himself. He is sitting there looking out the damn window thinking how he has wasted his whole life peddling milk. I figured what would a poor slob like that like to hear? How about a story about a kid who spent his entire childhood dreaming of becoming just like him? He had probably been sitting staring out that window all morning. Hasn't had an applicant in three weeks. He probably has nothing to tell his wife when he gets home from work every night. Tonight when he goes home he'll have this great story about a boy who always dreamed of becoming a milkman."

"So you made the guy's day?"

"Why not? What else am I doing? I'm unemployed, remember."

And how could anybody ever forget the Cushman Bakery delivery man and the tinkling bell of the ice cream truck, or the block ice delivery man. He had those huge ice tongs and that leather sheath he threw over his shoulder. I have since been told George Layland doubled in the summer as an ice man. That guy was a classic. And last but not least, there was the knife sharpening guy.

The knife sharpening guy had his own rig. He was another very old man. He had a wheelbarrow type thing he pushed down the street. He had a chant also but I don't recall how it went. In place of the carry bucket on his wheelbarrow he had a giant stone wheel. As I remember the big stone was white in color. I remember my mother frantically searching out every dull knife in the silverware drawer, sticking them into a paper bag or wrapping them up in a towel and sending me out in a run after the old man and his giant stone. I guess the "don't run with scissors" admonition was also after my time. Of course, children were a good deal cheaper in those days.

This guy had a neat business though, I loved to watch him. First he would set his wheelbarrow down and then he would flip back this buggy seat he had folded over at the handle end of the barrow. He would climb up into his buggy seat and then put his feet on the bicycle peddles he had hooked up to his stone. He would peddle his stone and get it rotating and then start edging the knives. It was neat to watch him. He had a rhythmic pace to his peddling and scraping. He also had a water bottle and he poured water onto his rotating wheel occasionally.

He would test the knives for sharpness by touching his thumb along the edge. When I would get the knives home both my mother and I would test a knife edge as the old man had done and invariably we would each cut our thumbs.

I remember examining that old man's thumb each time I brought him knives. He had a mean looking thumb, man, let me tell you. Wow, if thumbs could talk. That thumb had obviously been to hell and back.

Hey, somebody ought to write a book with that title "To Hell and Back." That would be a million seller, I'll bet.

PS – Don't write. I know all about Audie Murphy.

Jimmy and His Dog Tige

Jimmy was my good buddy Jack's older brother. I think Jimmy was only a year or so older than Jack. Jack wasn't much on "words" but Jimmy was even less. Jimmy didn't talk at all.

In his younger days Jimmy was always getting into fights. I think it would be safe to say Jimmy, as a kid, had a "hair trigger." He would go off sometimes and nobody could tell "how come."

One day I beat Jimmy in a game of basketball in St. Rita's schoolyard. Jimmy grabbed me up by the front of my shirt and slammed me against the school building. I thought he was going to kill me. He was two or three years older than me and I was seriously confused as to what I had done.

He held me there with his fists wrapped up in my shirt and glared at me. His eyes were burning. I said, "What? What's wrong? What did I do, Jimmy?"

He dropped me and left the schoolyard without saying a word. Jack was there with me. I said, "Jack what's bugging him?"

Jack said, "Don't mind him. He just doesn't like losing."

As time went on, I watched Jimmy get into other skirmishes with more skilled basketball players. I told Jack, "You know, your brother shouldn't really play basketball if he is going to beat the crap out of everybody who beats him in a game of one on one – either that or he

133

is going to have to get a lot better at basketball himself."
Jack laughed.

I was always late for high school — well grammar school
also. I was running through the parking lot passed
Kennedy's pool and then along the fence that separated
Central Catholic from the old city jail. I was huffing and
puffing and rushing as fast as I could up the hill, when I
heard a voice. "Hey Nobes! Nobes!" I turned and looked
around and it was one of the inmates at the city jail calling
me. Who the heck would I know that's in the city jail? It
was Jimmy.

"Hey Jimmy, what the hell you doing in there?"

"Aw … just some bullshit. Hey, do you have an extra
cigarette?" I had a half a pack of Camels in my pocket. I
said, "Here, take the whole pack."

"No, no," he said. "I'll just take two."

That's what always intrigued me about Jimmy. He had
this philosophy going on in his head. He never took stuff.
He was always fair — except if he lost. He laughed a lot —
at nothing. He would just look at you and then laugh. I
offered him the whole pack and he only took two. I
insisted he take them all but he would have none of it — a
Jimmy principle of moral character.

When I got my first grown-up, full-time job at S. H.
Brennan's Meat Packing, Jimmy was working there. He
taught me how to drive the truck and helped me learn all
the routes. After work we would go have a few beers
together.

Having a few beers with Jimmy was an experience. As I
have said, he didn't talk. We would sit at the bar and stare
into the mirror on the wall. Jimmy would look in the
mirror and see me looking at him in the glass and he
would laugh. "Want to go to Tubby Clark's?" he'd ask.

"Sure."

Spending an evening drinking with Jimmy was an
evening of thought and contemplation. Kind of like having

a dog – or being a dog, I don't know which. "Hi, I'm Buster Brown. I live in a shoe. This is my dog Tige. He lives in there too." It was peculiar but after a while I got used to it.

The basic idea was to keep moving. I never knew what Jimmy was looking for but when we didn't find it at one place we went to another. Periodically during the evening he would look at me and then laugh. I'd say, "Something funny about my face or what?"

He'd say, "Let's go to the Arlington Club." So off we'd go – bar hopping. Jimmy was restless. I was happy to have company – words or no words.

I would see Jack and I'd say, "Went bar hopping with your brother last night."

"Oh really? What did he have to say?"

"What did he have to say? You mean Jimmy speaks? Does Jimmy talk to you?"

"Not really. But I can tell when he is screwed up or not. You know what I mean?"

"Not at all. I just sit there. I've got my own game going now. I try to beat him to the punch and suggest the next bar before he does."

"Are you winning?"

"No, but I've tied a couple of times."

Jimmy had this world going on in his mind and it was obviously funny and filled with principles – Jimmy principles.

We were off in Beverly somewhere. Jimmy was teaching me the North Shore truck delivery route for S.H. Brennan's Meat Packing. After two' or three hours of silence he speaks, "Screw this, I've never gone this way before but this traffic is too much. I'm going to take a short cut." We wound around one tiny road after another. Jimmy was driving about 50 miles per hour in a 25 mile an hour zone. Our 12 or 13 foot high box, rail truck with 10 tons of swinging beef was bobbing and weaving. The truck felt as though we were riding on two wheels half the time.

We rounded a bend and then directly in front of us sat a railroad bridge. All Brennan drivers were warned about railroad bridges. They are low. They can rip the roof right off your truck. A driver had to be sure to know the height of his truck and the allowable height of the bridge. A warning sign was pasted to the dashboard of every truck along with the official height of the truck. "Oh shit!" said Jimmy and he jammed on the breaks. We slowed down to a crawl. There was a dip in the road running under the railroad bridge. From where we were the bridge appeared to be about four feet below the level of our front bumper. "Do you think we can make it under that bridge?"

"Are you crazy? Not a chance. You will not only rip the top of this truck off but it looks to me that bridge is low enough to rip both of our heads off too. You better stop and back up."

"Screw it! I'm going for it." And Jimmy hit the gas. The truck leaped forward then dipped down the hill before the bridge. I hit the floor and braced myself for the impact. Zip ... we came out on the other side with no problem."

I unfolded my arms from around my head and looked up from the floor of the truck at Jimmy. He laughed.

We were off to the Marblehead Store. This store got ten or twelve cattle – in quarters. That meant each piece weighted about 200 pounds and we had to carry every piece about ten miles to get it to the back door of the meat market.

Backing in was another story. There was a small alley almost as wide as the truck – well maybe slightly wider. On one side of the alley was a package store and on the other side was a gift shop. Jimmy immediately started laughing.

"Want me to get out and direct you in?" I asked.

"No, not really. I'll get us some help."

Bamb, bamb! Jimmy bounces off one wall and then the other as he attempted to back into the alley. The guy from the package store was out in the street in nothing flat and then the lady from the gift store appeared for the opposing team. They each started giving directions. The lady signaled with her hands and screamed, "More the other way!" Bamb! We're bouncing off the package store wall.

The package store guy yells, "No, no, the other way!" Bamb bamb! We're bouncing off the gift shop wall. Jimmy has his serious face on like he is really trying not to hit anything. I'm shaking my head. I've seen Jimmy back down a winding, impossible alley in Boston and then in between two other trucks with barely an inch to spare and not ever hit anything. He's busting balls – or whiskey bottles and tea cups. He looked at the lady, "That way?" he pantomimed, questioningly from behind the wheel of the truck.

"Yes, yes!" she screamed, nodding her head up and down in anxious agreement. "That way!"

"No no," screamed the package store guy. "The other F'in way you moron. Where did you get your license, Sears and Roebucks?"

Oops, package store guy loses. Bamb bamb!

The tail end of our truck finally hit the loading ramp. Now Jimmy was really going to hear about it, I figured. He was going to have to pass right by the two store owners to get around the corner to the meat market entrance.

But wait a minute. I tried to open my door. The walls were so close the doors didn't open. Jimmy rolled down his window, scootched out through the window and then slithered up onto the roof of the cab. Naturally my window was busted and wouldn't roll down – as if Jimmy didn't know that. I must bungle over all the Dixie cups and tonic bottles to the driver's side of the cab, then scootch out the window and up onto the roof of the cab behind Jimmy. From the cab roof we climb onto the refrigeration compressor unit to the roof of the box truck. It is then, over the roof, hang from the back of the box by the fingertips and drop to the platform below. Upon landing Jimmy looked at me and after a slight pause, laughed.

"You really think that is F'n funny, don't you?"

And every time we returned to the Marblehead store Jimmy did the same thing. On one occasion he had this big heavy kid with him as a helper. The kid weighed over 250 pounds. The poor boy almost had a heart attack, I was told – and that was just going under the railroad bridge, never mind squeezing out the window and climbing up and over the truck.

I thought of Jimmy as a mental challenge. I was, like the "Jimmy Whisperer." I had to learn the secret "Jimmy language."

Jimmy was uncontrollable, non-communicative, unpredictable, secretive, and explosive but once you got into his "style" he could be very funny – in a dangerous sort of way.

I always liked traveling with him. It was quiet but intriguing. It was a way for me to get off by myself but yet not be alone.

The English Social Club

The English Social Club was one of a million such places in Lawrence: the French Social, the Polish National, the Irish Social, the German American, the Sons of Italy and on and on and on. Needless to say, these were all barrooms of one nature or another. Barrooms and churches, corner variety stores, sandwich shops, poolrooms and back alleys, mills and smoke stacks, penny candy and 10 cent Bea's sauce sandwiches – Lawrence, my hometown.

There was a small duckpin bowling alley in the back of the English Social, five or six lanes I guess. How the "gang" and I incorporated ourselves as the official pin boys at the English Social Club is a matter of debate.

My recollection is that me and some of the guys were playing stickball out in the back parking lot. Jimmy Bowan was pitching to Busty Royle. Busty had brought it to a full count. Jimmy says, "Okay, now this is getting serious." He takes off his T-shirt and drapes it over the trunk of a parked car. He returns to the mound and proceeds to go through all the motions and shenanigans of a major league pitcher. He zings one right down the pike. Busty swings and fouls it off. Jimmy gets the ball back and commences in a Bob Feller manner. Busty decides to throw him off balance. He holds up a hand indicating a break in the action. He steps back from the plate and pulls his T-shirt up over his head and tosses it over on a section of broken telephone pole that was lying over by the back of the garage that we were using as a backstop. Busty returns to the plate. Jimmy winds up, then bends over and stares down towards the plate – pretending to be getting his signals from the catcher.

"Wait a minute! Wait a Minute!" Jimmy says stepping off the mound. "I ain't throwing another pitch until you get that damn rat off your shoulder."

"What the hell are you talking about?" Busty inquires, dubiously.

"I'm talking about that damn raccoon or whatever it is that you got covering your damn shoulder. What the hell is that damn thing?"

"You mean this?" Busty says pointing to what looks to be a beaver pelt or some kind of animal flopped over his left shoulder.

"Yeah! That's right. Whatever that is, get it off your shoulder. It's distracting me. You can't have a damn dead cat over your shoulder while a guy is trying to pitch. That's against the rules."

"This ain't no dead cat. And I can't take it off my shoulder. It's a birthmark."

"Birthmark, my ass. That's a birth territory, or a birth continent. A birthmark is a small dot, a pimple or a little splash of color. A birthmark don't cover two thirds of someone's body. Stop breaking chops and get that fur coat off your shoulder or I ain't pitching."

"It doesn't come off. Now come on and just pitch."

"Oh no! Oh no, no, no, no! ... Sheehy!" Jimmy screams to our honorary commissioner of behind-the-garage stickball. "Check that thing out. If it ain't real, make him get it off there, or I ain't pitching."

Jack Sheehy strolls over to the plate. He examines Busty's shoulder. He looks it over very closely. "It's the real thing, all right. It's a mole or something. It is a giant, goddamn mole or something."

Jimmy Bowan drops the ball on the mound. "It can't be. I don't believe it. I gotta see this." Pretty soon there is a crowd around Busty. Everybody is ohh-ing and ahh-ing. Nobody can believe their eyes.

"You know Frankie Speers has six toes on each of his feet. Did any of you guys ever see that?"

"Six toes? You're kidding? Nobody can have six toes. God doesn't do things like that."

"Didn't you ever see one of them freaks at the circus?"

"That's baloney! They just make them up to look like that. It's a trick. It's all phony."

"Well what is that slab of goop on Busty's damn shoulder then?"

"That's something Busty just put there. I'll bet it peels off. Look, grab a piece of that thing and pull."

At just about the time that one of the guys was about to grab hold of Busty's birthmark and rip it off, a little bald-headed guy poked his head out of the back door to the English Social Club and said; "Any of you kids want to make some money?"

We all rushed to the back door and pushed and shoved our way in behind the short, fat, bald-headed guy. He led us through some swinging doors and into the bowling alley. We were all excited. We were not only excited about the thought of earning some money but about being allowed into a barroom. There were too many of us for the number of alleys so we decided to take turns. We would each set up one string and then sit out and give another guy a shot at setting up a string.

We started walking down the center of the alley and instantly all the men began yelling at us. "You gotta walk down the gutters. You can't walk on the lanes, you boneheads. Them lanes is all polished up. You'll get 'em all scuffed. Don't you guys know nothin'!" We all scurried

141

over into the gutters. Some of us guys even took off our shoes.

This was exciting. This was almost like a real job. There were rules to it and everything. That's what makes something important, you know – rules. Things with rules to them are more important than things without rules. No walking down the middle of the alley – that was a good one. Like it mattered to this group of "professional" duck pin bowlers if the lanes were polished or not. In an hour or two of downing 10 cent beers any of these guys will be lucky if they can roll a ball and hit any one of the several different lanes never mind a pin – with or without a kid's sneaker print scuffing up the polished finish.

Okay, so there I am at the bottom of a bowling alley. The pins are all lying in the hole behind me. On the lane in front of me are a bunch of round black circles. The circles are set down in the shape of a diamond. Very simple – put the pins on the circles. Then you jump up onto a bench that is behind the hole. The guy up at the front of the lane throws the ball down the lane. The ball hits the pins. The pins fly all over hell and you learn to duck and cover your head. I figured that was why they called them "duck" pins. Every time the ball hit them, the pin boy had to duck.

As the men who were bowling got drunker and drunker, it seemed that they purposely tried to catch the pin boy before he got out of the hole and up onto his perch. You had to put that last pin onto the black spot and then run for your life. There was no dallying around in the "black hole." If you weren't paying attention or you dallied too long, you'd be ducking duckpins right and left. They were heavy suckers too. If you wanted the job you couldn't bitch about getting hit by the flying pins – that was all a part of it.

If you wanted that ten cents a string, you had to tolerate the drunken shenanigans of the fathead bowlers

142

too. After all, they were the adults. If you complained, they called you a sissy and told you to go home. Home was never the place any of us guys wanted to be.

In retribution for the bowlers throwing the bowling balls ninety miles an hour and trying to catch us in the pit behind the alleys, we stationed some of our little people up in the bowlers' territory. It was the duty of these "scouts" to steal glasses of draft beer off the various tables and hide them under the line of folding chairs at the back of the hall when the bowlers weren't watching. Between all the pilfered glasses of beer under the chairs and the half-full glasses left on the tables at the end of the night, we had a party each and every night.

I can still remember the taste of that first beer. It was strange, bitter, warm and flat – but at least it had no cigarette butts floating in it. Nevertheless, it was the fruit from the forbidden tree. And it was ever so sweet, especially when followed by the sinful, exotic, smoky flavor of a Lucky Strike or Camel cigarette. If I close my eyes, I can taste and feel it all. Ah yes, those were the days. How I managed to live this long, is the 64,000 dollar question.

Jasper Smith

Jasper Smith was the only black kid I ever knew growing up in Lawrence. Another buddy, Willie Laird, has recently informed me that he was a Hispanic – I guess he still is. Willie's mother was supposedly the first Hispanic woman in Lawrence, arriving sometime in the 40's. I knew Willie's mother spoke a foreign language but so did my grandmother. Most of my buddies had a parent or grandparent who spoke some "jibber-jabber" also – who cared.

We had no "black problem" in Lawrence when I was growing up, nor did we have a Hispanic problem. We really didn't have any racial or ethnic problems – not us kids anyway. For our parents, it was not so easy.

Though my Polack mother would never acknowledge it, my Irish father was shut off from his siblings because of his marriage choice.

I met Jasper at the St. Rita's schoolyard basketball court. It was very dark. The streetlight in front of Plonowski's Funeral Parlor was out. It was so dark that I was only shooting lay-ups. I saw a kid walking through the schoolyard from Arlington St. He was silhouetted by the streetlight on the corner of Arlington and Hampshire. With the light at his back, all I saw was a figure. When he got to the court he asked if I wanted to play a little one on one. I said sure and tossed him the ball. As he dribbled the ball with his back to me, I noticed he had funny hair. When he spun around to take a jump shot, I saw he was black. This was the closest I had ever been to a black person in my life. I was in the sixth or seventh grade. I was eleven or twelve years old. That would make the year 1954 or 1955. The modern day Black Civil Rights Movement was heating up. I had seen black people on TV but never had I seen one up close and personal.

It turned out that Jasper lived at the end of Arlington St. towards Broadway. Since I lived on Chelmsford St. we walked home together. We passed my pro-model Voit basketball back and forth and dribbled up the center of Arlington St. The Voit basketball had that hard leather clunking sound when it hit the pavement. I didn't like the balls that had that spongy "boing" rubber sound – very unprofessional.

It was dark with a streetlight working here and there. Kids often threw rocks at the dangling, unprotected, streetlight bulbs putting them out of commission. When they were busted they buzzed like a giant cricket. The city finally caught on and covered the bulbs with a difficult to break, hard, glass dome cover.

There were no cars and no people on the street. It was after 9 o'clock – it was late. My new buddy told me on our walk home that his name was John Smith but that everybody called him Jasper.

I remember being very curious. Every time we got under a streetlight that was working I took a closer look. I can still remember how fascinated I was to see a person whose skin was actually black – I mean black, not brown or tanned or olive. Jasper had dark black skin. It was shocking to me. I could hardly believe it. I don't know why I felt this way but I remember these feelings distinctly. It was kinda like discovering that Frankie Squires had six toes or Nancy Sullivan had an extra "baby" finger.

The next day when I went to school, the nun gave us a serious speech. None of the other kids knew what she was talking about. But I knew.

She spoke of "different" types of people and how all people are to be treated equal. She was very serious and it was clear she was nervous. Specifically, she mentioned we would be having a new kid in our class and this kid would be "different" from the rest of us and we should treat her with kindness and respect. The little, black girl in my class was Jasper's younger sister. I don't remember her name. Jasper was a grade or two above me.

Jasper's sister stayed at our school only a day or two – I think she felt smothered. All the other girls doted on her as if she were a celebrity. Jasper loved the attention so he hung in at St. Rita's. Everybody wanted to be Jasper's friend. He had a party.

He played on the grammar school basketball league as we all did. What I remember most was his underwear. He didn't wear jockey shorts. He wore similar type shorts but they were longer. When he ran around on the court his underwear would slip down below his uniform trunks. Nobody else in the entire league had an underwear problem like Jasper's. But nobody said anything. Everybody noticed, but nobody said a word. Jasper was the toast of our little white kiddy world – and he loved it.

He hung out at Nell's with us on the Corner. Whenever the cops would come and start taking names and Jasper told them his name was John Smith they would get extremely upset. The rest of us would always come to Jasper's defense. "He ain't lyin'. That's his name, John Smith. And he never met Pocahontas either."

On occasion the cops wouldn't believe us and they would take Jasper over and throw him into the back of the cruiser. But while they continued taking our names one of us would always sneak over to the cruiser and "bust" Jasper out. Jasper would take off running and they could never catch him. After a few months most of the cops accepted "John Smith" as legitimate and went along with their usual and customary intimidation.

He would come over to my house and play basketball in my backyard with the rest of us from St. Rita's Pintos, Ponies or Mustangs. My Uncle Ray had set up a basket on the top of the garages behind our tenement. We would open the garage doors under the basket so we could drive in for lay-ups. My uncle didn't always have all the garages rented out, so that stall was usually empty. I will never forget the expressions on my relatives' faces the first time they saw Jasper playing in their backyard. To say the least he stuck out like a chocolate in a bowl of marshmallows.

Jasper was also a boxer and everybody seemed to know him. A bunch of us were walking home from the boy's club across from the Common on Haverhill St. one night and as we passed the St. Mary's auditorium just before Hampshire St. a man came popping out the door. There was a special event going on. This man called to Jasper.

"Hey, Jasper, you are just the guy I'm looking for. One of my fighters didn't show up. How about you filling in for me?"

The rest of us didn't know what was going on. He was asking Jasper to fight in the Silver Mittens or some such thing. Jasper really wasn't interested, but we all went nuts.

Because we got Jasper to volunteer for this guy, the man let us all in for free to watch the fights. This was the first "professional" boxing match I had ever seen.

Jasper won on a unanimous decision and we all cheered like crazy. His opponent was really terrible. He danced around the ring for the entire first round and Jasper had to chase him all over. Finally Jasper caught him with a good one. The other kid got totally offended. He put his boxing mitts onto his hips, stood with his shoulders back and his chin jutting out and said, "Oh, you want to fight

147

huh?" Everyone in the audience turned and looked at one another and then burst out laughing. But from that moment on he was chopped meat. He dispensed with all he had learned and began running into Jasper with his arms flailing. Jasper stayed cool and boxed the hell out of him.

Jasper eventually moved out of Lawrence and went to Lowell or Haverhill. He was still just a teenager when he got killed in a terrible car accident. He was messed up so badly his parents kept the casket closed.

The funeral parlor was filled with white and black people. Jasper had as many white friends as he had black buddies. He was a super friendly kid. He was only a snapshot in my life but his brief appearance remains bright and clear in my reverie to this day – and we are talking over 50 years past. He was certainly more than a pair of drooping underwear. We did many things together and shared many laughs. He laughed constantly.

After the first encounter at St. Rita's I don't ever remember thinking about his black skin in the same way. It didn't go away or rub off, but all in all he was just like the rest of us in Lawrence – all the same yet all quite different.

Billy Kaeton is going to Hell

Billy Kaeton looked like a normal kid. He had wandered down from north of the Howard. He was actually from Methuen. Kids from Methuen were OK. We had a number of guys in the Corner gang who were from Methuen.

Methuen kids weren't like the regular Lawrence guys. Some of them didn't even live in a tenement house. They actually lived in a house where nobody other than their immediate family lived. Methuen guys were considered more wealthy and somewhat pampered and spoiled compared to us Lawrence kids. But us guys from Lawrence weren't bigots. We were an equal opportunity gang.

Billy Kaeton's dad was a doctor and they lived a few blocks north of the Howard Playground in a single family ranch home. One day I walked him home. He stopped at this fancy styled ranch house that was surrounded by a split rail "designer" fence. When we got to his place, he invited me in. I thought he was busting my chops. Nobody in our gang lived in a house like that. Everyone I knew lived in an apartment. And everybody's apartment was pretty much alike. I figured he was pulling a fast one on me. I decided to call his bluff. I figured by the time we reached the front door, he would come clean, we would both have a big laugh, and then go to his real house.

We got to the front door and he opened it and walked inside. I nearly flipped out. I still figured he was busting chops and he had just opened the door to this strange rich person's house. Now we would really be in trouble. He motioned for me to follow him. I didn't move. I stood outside the entrance and gawked at the inside like a stray cat exploring new, untested territory.

"Come on! Let's go to my bedroom and play with some of my toys," he said.

What in the world was this kid talking about? Let's go to "his" bedroom and play with some of "his toys." What was this, the land of Little Lord Fauntleroy, or what? This kid had his own room and he had toys in his room?

I came to the conclusion that he actually lived there. I followed but very tentatively. The inside of the house looked like something out of a storybook to me. I felt like an aborigine who had just dropped from the jungle into Grand Central Station. I was looking everywhere except where I was going. I kept bumping into everything.

We walked through a fancy entrance-way and then into a big room. All the floors were covered in thick carpeting – even the hallway. I kept thinking I should take my shoes off or something. Billy kept chanting, "Come on! Come on!"

There was someone reading a newspaper, sitting in a big leather chair in front of a huge fireplace. I had never seen anything like this in my life.

The man in the chair peeked from behind his paper and over his reading glasses. When he saw me, he folded up the paper and called out to Billy as he stepped in front of my path and latched onto my arm. He smiled as he escorted me back to the entrance and scooted me back out the door. I felt like I had just got caught by the usher at the Palace Theater after sneaking in the back entrance.

He closed the door. I was standing outside by myself. I heard Billy inside whining to his father that I was his new friend and he brought me home to play with his toys in his bedroom. I heard his dad say, "I want to meet any new friends you make before you bring them home. That boy is obviously trouble. All I need is one look and I know that. What is the matter with you?"

I didn't wait for Billy to come out and talk to me. I just figured his dad was pissed. I walked back down to the Howard and then down the hill to Nell's Variety.

I didn't tell any of the other guys about the incident even when Billy showed up down at Nell's the next day. I think I was a little ashamed that his father just looked at me and thought I was trouble. I thought I looked pretty much like all the other guys.

The first thing Billy did was apologize. He said his dad was just grumpy. I told him that was what I figured. He proceeded to make friends with some of the other guys. Everybody liked him. He was very friendly and outgoing – but Billy was different ... really different.

He had been hanging around at Nell's with us for a couple of weeks when someone mentioned that most of us usually met at King Tut's on Sunday mornings before we headed off for the eight o'clock mass at St. Mary's or the Immaculate Conception. He then mentioned that he was not a Roman Catholic but an Episcopalian.

Oh my, the silence was deafening. None of us could believe it. We all looked him over more closely – and with great sympathy. Not a one of us had ever seen a live person who we knew was definitely going to hell. There was one hope. Maybe he was like those pygmies in Africa or someplace who had never heard of the one true Church.

Someone squeaked out squeamishly, "Did you ever hear of the Roman Catholic Church?"

"Of course I have."

Humm, bad news! He knew about the one true Church and he didn't care. It was over. Unfortunately our new friend Billy whose father was a rich doctor who lived in a fancy house up in Methuen was going to hell. Wow! Ain't that something, we all thought. It's just like we were taught in St. Rita's. "What good does it do a man to gain the whole world and end up losing his soul."

I don't know which one of us it was who broke the news to Billy but somebody had to do it.

"You do know that you are going to hell."

"I am not."

"Oh yes you are. You know about the Roman Catholic Church and you refuse to join. That means you are going to hell."

"Other religions can all go to heaven besides Roman Catholics."

"'Fraid not, Billy-boy. Whoever told you that one?"

"The priest at my church."

"You ain't got no real priest at your church. If he ain't Catholic, he ain't no priest."

"He is so!"

"Sorry buddy, the priest at your church is an imposter. He's going to hell too; you can bet on that."

Billy got really, really upset when he learned the truth. None of us thought all that much about it. We had to tell him. When a kid is going to hell, he should know about it.

Billy returned the next day fortified with information he got from this phony priest who belonged to this phony church.

He started telling us about these popes who were bad guys in ancient times. We told him we knew all that crap. And we knew about Episcopalians too. "Your church was started by this whacko King of England who wanted to divorce one of his wives. He was a big, stupid, fat guy. All he wanted to do was eat and screw pretty Queens. When the Pope wouldn't give him a divorce, he started his own phony church and chopped his wife's head off. You mean to tell us you are going to put your faith in a nutcake like that?"

He babbled on about the Pope and burning people at the stake and all this ancient history stuff. Who cared! That was all a long time ago. And most of all this anti-Catholic garble was made up by a bunch of clowns who just didn't like keeping the commandments and living like respectable Catholics. At one time everybody was Roman Catholic until all these perverts like this King Henry came along, we told him.

The next day when he came back he told us his priest had told him Roman Catholics were crazy and they hated everybody and wanted to destroy all the people who didn't think like they did.

We laughed. "That is ridiculous. Listen, if you and your whacky priest want to go to hell, go ahead. We were just trying to help you out because we like you and you seem like a nice kid. But if you choose to go to hell, go with your eyes open. Don't fool yourself."

"Well, Father Bob says Roman Catholics are dangerous and they have guns stored in all the cellars of their churches."

"Oh wow! Father Bob is it? Well tell "Father Bob" we will bring him down to the cellar of any Catholic Church and if he finds anything other than scribbled over, losing bingo cards and angel food, cake crumbs from the last bake sale, we'll buy him a free season ticket to Canobe Lake Park."

Billy got all red in the face. He didn't know what to say but what could he say? It is tough to have the truth thrown right in your face. Unfortunately, Billy will just have to deal with it, we thought.

We watched him walk up the hill towards the Howard. We felt really sorry for him. He never came back to the corner and we never saw him again. But he was the only kid any of us ever met, face to face, who we knew for certain was going to hell.

Since that time I have met many, many sad, uninformed souls who will be going to hell. Unfortunately one of them is my wife. She says she is a Methodist. I have asked her what method the Methodists believe in. She doesn't know and she doesn't really care. She says she liked being a Methodist as a child because of the sauerkraut suppers and the "nifflies" they served up in the cellars of their churches. Nifflies are boiled noodle dough drenched in real butter and salt. I asked her if she thought Catholics had guns in the cellars of their churches. She said she didn't think so.

I have never told her she is going to hell – though I must admit, I have come very close many, many times.

Father Kelley

My wife constantly accuses me of having a moral conscience. She has learned over the years about all my friends, my family, relatives and whatever. She has come to the conclusion that none of the above contributed much to the development of my "moral conscience." She suggests the only influence in my life that could be responsible for this moral conscience she thinks I have, must be the Roman Catholic Church.

For the longest time me and my street corner buddies went to Confession every Friday night. If St. Mary's Church had two hundred people inside on a Friday night waiting to tell their confessions to a priest, 90% of them would be lined up at Father Kelley's confessional. Father Kelley was a very kind and forgiving man and in his role as a priest he was equally generous with God's graces. No matter how grievous a transgression you may have confessed, Father Kelley would say: "Are you truly sorry that you have committed such a deed?"

"Yes Father, I am."

"As your penance say three Our Fathers and three Hail Marys. Go in peace, my son."

This, of course, was the reason for the long line at Father Kelley's confessional every week.

On this one particular Friday night a priest who was waiting alone and lonely inside his little cubicle on the

155

empty side of the church, stepped out of his anonymity and gave a speech to all us reluctant confessors.

He accused us of cowardice. Certainly we all couldn't have committed such outrageous sins that we were afraid of an objective consequence or penance. He advised us to remember that all our penance and suffering here on earth would be to our credit once we arrived in heaven. He also insinuated that all priests were forgiving and compassionate by nature.

Several older people rose from their pews but instead of walking over to our admonisher's side of the church, they walked out the side door. They could come back later after things cooled down a little and reposition themselves at Father Kelley's station.

The chastising priest shook his head in disgust and returned to his stall.

I sat there thinking about what the priest had said and I concluded that certainly with my little, dinky sins I should not be afraid to kneel before any Roman Catholic priest.

After about fifteen or twenty minutes of analysis and soul searching, I left the safety and security of my pew at Father Kelley's station and meandered over to the other side of the church.

Naturally there was still no one there, so I stepped right up to the plate.

As a part of my confession, I admitted to this priest I had been stealing penny candy from Dube's Variety store which was on the corner of Chelmsford and Center Streets. He was shocked. He wanted to know why I did that. I stuttered and stammered.

This had never happened at father Kelley's station. He never said boo. He never asked "why" I did anything. He would say, "Three Our Fathers and three Hail Marys," and that was the end of it. Now this new guy was asking "why?" What was this? Is that a fair question for a priest to ask in a confessional? Was this a pop quiz or what?

"I don't know why I took the penny candy Father. I guess I just wanted it."

"Well son, as your penance I want you to go back to Dube's Variety store. I want you to apologize and I want you to pay her back for all the candy you stole."

OH MY GOD! What had I done? I was certainly heartily sorry for leaving father Kelley's station. And certainly, I will never do that again! But now what do I do?

Would it count if I went back over to Father Kelley and told him the same sins over and got three Our Fathers and three Hail Marys – like I knew he would give me? Would I have to tell Father Kelley I had been across the way to this other priest?

I went back to Father Kelley and he did just as I suspected he would, but yet the whole situation plagued me. One day I gathered up all my pennies and went up to Dube's Variety. I was trembling as I entered through her screen door. As usual it took her five minutes to get to the counter. I could have stolen a pocket full of candy by then – but I didn't.

When she got to the counter, I laid down all my pennies and confessed. Mrs. Dube stared at me like I was a kid who had just landed on the planet earth from outer space. She scooped up the pennies and eventually sputtered, "You are an admirable young man."

All the way back to my house I questioned if it was better to be a known thief and an "admirable young man" or to have remained anonymous and said three Our Fathers and three Hail Marys.

From that day forward I took my errands to Walter's Variety on the corner down the hill on Center St. How could I ever face Mrs. Dube again, the little thief from down the block on Chelmsford St? I never stole anything at Walter's. I wasn't about to go through that again.

Graduation

Jimmy Rowland had a 1953 Mercury. He lived on Spruce St. and I lived one block over on Chelmsford. I met Jimmy in my early Walter's Variety Store period. I think I may have been guilty of teaching him how to smoke cigarettes.

I can still remember the afternoon when Dickey Bolton taught me how to inhale. Very shortly thereafter, I was puffing out smoke rings and filtering smoke out through my nose. If only physics or algebra gave me the same thrill.

Jimmy got his faded blue '53 Merc just in time for our junior year at Central Catholic High School. He had a plan for the interior but only got so far as to remove the bolts that secured the front seat to the floor.

Jimmy was always late. I was always late too, but Jimmy was often even later. I would sit out on my front porch waiting as long as I dared for his Merc to turn the corner. By two or three minutes after eight I had to start hoofing it, Jimmy or no Jimmy.

Most often by the time I hit Arlington St. or Henry's (DeSantas's) Variety on Spruce St., Jimmy would race up beside me and honk. I would jump in the front passenger side, voicing my relief and discontent. Jimmy would apologize for being late. He would put his cigarette between his lips and grab onto the steering wheel with both hands, then laugh and hit the gas. Without fail the

158

front seat would flop backwards, and I would go ass over tea kettle into the backseat.

Every damn morning, it was the same thing. I still can't believe that I could never realize what was going to happen and brace myself accordingly. I was always so worried about being late and getting 11 years in room 22 from Vice Principal Marcel, Brother Herman Goering, or whatever his name was. He had replaced Brother Richard who was great. This new guy and his pal, Principal Huge (Adolf) Ephram or whatever, Brother George's replacement, were, in my opinion, responsible for the pussifying of Central Catholic High School.

They were trying to turn it from a rough and tumble Lawrence neighborhood school into some kind of fancy conservatory or Ivy League prep school. I was totally opposed to the reconstruction.

The orchestrated cheering practices with the cheers actually spelled out on a piece of paper were too much for me – Rah, rah, rah, sis boom bah. I couldn't believe it. Today they even have "girls" attending Central Catholic. My God! Total pussification!

I don't know where Jimmy got his wardrobe but he had some wild ties and shirts – and he wore them to school every day.

He had a variety of Hawaiian, multicolored pastel shirts – sky blue, turquoise, pink, sunset yellow, pacific green and several other bright "pretty" colors splashed randomly over the fabric. He would top this type shirt off with a wide flaring tie – usually sporting a girl in a bikini or a guy on a surfboard. He had some ties where one could turn the tie this way or that way and the girl would change bikinis or the wave would crash on the surfboarding guy. I don't remember if he had any ties that glowed in the dark or lit up in psychedelic colors – but he may have.

The brothers always took note of Jimmy's choice in attire but no one said anything. Hawaii was a state, you know. I suppose it could have been considered unpatriotic to criticize. Jimmy's dad could have been an admiral stationed at Pearl Harbor or something – you never know.

Brother Joe, the freshmen football coach, caught us coming down the second floor gym corridor "almost" late one morning. Brother Joe noticed Jimmy's shirt and tie and seemed to be displeased. He stopped Jimmy but to my surprise only asked that Jimmy tuck the shirt into his pants. He made no comment on the hula girl tie or the blazing sunset shirt. Jimmy sighed deeply, tucked in the front of his shirt but not the sides or the back and hurried off.

Brother Joe was not entirely satisfied with that response. He grabbed Jimmy by the back of the shirt and slammed him up against the cold, cement block wall. With his nose nearly touching Jimmy's nose he said in a quiet determined anger, "What do you think you are, a smart guy?" Brother Joe sounded very much like Edward G. Robinson in one of those gangster movies or Clint Eastwood in a "make my day" sort of way.

"No Bruddah. You said to tuck my shirt in. So I did."

"You did huh. Is that how you always tuck in your shirt to attend classes here at Central Catholic High?"

"No Bruddah, but I was in a rush. We're a little late today."

"Tuck in the shirt properly," Brother Joe threatened while releasing his stranglehold on Jimmy throat.

Jimmy followed instructions and was released but the warning bell sounded. By the "rule" everybody had to be in their homeroom by the sounding of the warning bell. If not, a possible 11 years in room 22, standing at attention and staring at the back wall, if caught by the Gestapo.

I had scurried into our homeroom. I was safe. Jimmy was late and suddenly there stood Brother Herman Goering at our homeroom door. Jimmy was done for – but

160

not quite. He snuck up behind the Brother and waited. With a little luck, maybe he could sneak passed.

The Brother had his arm stretched across the doorway. When the Brother turned his head to the left, Jimmy swayed to his right. When the Brother turned his head to the right, Jimmy swayed to the left. Everyone in the class was aware of the situation – even our homeroom brother, Simian, the school bus driver. The class began to laugh and mumble and everyone was looking toward Brother Herman Georing standing in the doorway with his shadow, Charlie Chaplin, bobbing and weaving behind him. The assistant principal finally got the message and he turned slowly to the left to see what might be going on behind him. As he did Jimmy slipped into the room via his right. Brother Georing did a complete pirouette but discovered nothing unusual. The classroom was in an uproar, even Brother Simian was laughing. Jimmy was safe and already fumbling with the combination lock on his locker.

Jimmy was also a lady's man. I can still remember the time he had one steady girlfriend at the front door of one of our beach cottages while entertaining another semi-steady girl in the kitchen. On that occasion he escaped via the bathroom window. The two steady girls passed one another at the door both looking for Jimmy but never met or spoke – and were none the wiser.

Now I'm telling you all this in preparation for graduation night. I could have simply said Jimmy was a funny fellow or a clown of sorts but that wouldn't have painted the proper picture. You should have Jimmy in your sights by now. So let us now return to that fateful evening in the Central High gymnasium.

We had practiced for this event a hundred times. There really was no reason for a problem. We knew who would be first and who would be last in each row. There should have been nothing to it. We had lined up on the gym floor. We all knew who was to be on our right and our left. We knew what direction each row would take on their path to get up and onto the stage where we would receive our diplomas. We even practiced taking our diploma in our LEFT hand and shaking hands with our right. We had gone through all of this, time after time. It should have been a piece of cake. And it was a piece of cake for the entire graduating class ... except for one individual.

There was only one thing we hadn't practiced. We did not practice with the actual folding chairs lined up on the gym floor. It was considered superfluous, I imagine.

Jimmy was supposed to be in the end seat on my row. But for some reason one clown in our row didn't scooch up to the guy next to him. When Jimmy attempted to assume his position in the last seat on the aisle in my row there was no space. Jimmy tried to push the kid who was standing in front of his folding chair in a bit but the guy wouldn't budge. Jimmy had to think and move quickly. The audience of parents and admirers was seated up above on the floor that looked down onto the gym. Everybody – all the parents and relatives – could see everything. They had an elevated bird's eye view of the gym floor.

Since the guy in front of Jimmy's seat wouldn't budge, Jimmy had to push his way into the line entering the row behind us.

I felt someone tapping on my shoulder. Jimmy was now sitting off to the right behind me. "That F'in butthole wouldn't push in," he whispered, terror struck.

"Yes, I noticed that," I whispered looking straight ahead.

"I'm going to kill that son-of-a-bee after this is over. What do I do now?"

"I have no idea."

"Everybody is going to get the wrong diplomas. Jez-zus F'in H. Christ! Can you believe this sh–t?"

I turned my head slightly to look at Jimmy's face. I had never before in our career together as friends seen Jimmy with such a distressed look. For reasons beyond my control a tiny sputter of laughter began to well up inside of my stomach. It felt kinda like a burp or gas or something. I tried to hold it down. But slowly it began gurgling out. I began sputtering in my seat. I kept my mouth closed but then my cheeks would puff up with suppressed chuckle and uncontrollable little noises began erupting from me. I couldn't stop them from coming out. I tried burying my face in my hands. I kept thinking this could only happen to Jimmy Rowland.

The guys on both sides of me started elbowing me. "Come on man! Our parents are here watching this. This is important you screw off."

I looked over to my left. Out of the corner of my eye I saw my buddy Peter. He was scrunched up onto one little folding chair with some other, big fat guy. He peeked down his row and saw Jimmy sitting there in the wrong place, and then he looked over at me. When he saw my face, my condition spread to him. His cheeks began to bubble up and then we were both sputtering and backfiring as we shook and rattled in our folding chairs.

I could feel Jimmy glaring at the back of my head. I turned and peeked ever so cautiously. Jimmy's face was extremely red. He tried to maintain his frowning temperament but looking at me it became difficult.

"This is not funny," he whispered with a slight giggle and a half grin that vanished almost before it started.

"I know, I'm sorry but I just can't help it," I whispered in return.

I realized that I couldn't look at Jimmy. I kept looking straight ahead and concentrating on the ceremony.

Next, I heard a small commotion behind me. I peeked over my shoulder for a second time and Jimmy was gone. I turned to my left and there was Jimmy crawling along the floor in the row behind me. All the guys in my row were now seated in their proper chair. Jimmy's end-of-the-row seat was miraculously vacant. Jimmy decided to get to his seat commando style. But he had a long crawl ahead of him. He had to go to the end of Peter's row and sneak around the corner into our row and then crawl all along the entire row of about twenty or thirty folding chairs, over everybody's spit-shined shoes, until he reached his proper seat at the other end.

As I watched him crawling down the aisle towards me on two knees and one hand – the other hand holding his graduation cap onto his head, I nearly went into a convulsion. I was sure everybody in the entire building could hear me gulping and puffing. I tried pretending that I was coughing but it was a strange sound.

When Jimmy finally arrived at my chair, he stopped and looked up at me – on his knees, one hand bracing the floor and the other holding his graduation cap to his head. The golden tassel dangled down between his eyes and over his nose. He tried to puff it out of his line of vision. It didn't budge. I thought I was going to die. I exploded. I turned my explosion into a rather strange sounding sneeze followed by some severe coughing and hiccupping. Students from all over were turning to look at me but it was beyond my control.

When Jimmy finally slid up onto his rightful seat at the end of our row with two dirty knee spots on his graduation gown, his face and neck traffic-light red, and glanced down in my direction, it was all over for me. The remainder of my graduation was a blur of tears, deep breaths, and failed attempts to control the "giggles" and the sputters. I remember nothing else from that afternoon. I don't even remember going up to the stage to get my diploma. I don't know who gave it to me. My whole graduation is Jimmy Rowland.

I never again saw Jimmy with as frightened and frustrated a face as he exhibited on that graduation day. Even at his wedding, he was less flustered. The only image that remains with me today of that entire graduation event, so important to everyone's life, is that of Jimmy Rowland crawling past me on the gymnasium floor and stopping to look up at me in utter desperation. If I only had one of our modern digital cameras, I could have captured the "look" of a lifetime. That one look made up for a thousand early morning tumbles into the backseat of that darn '53 Merc. Oh brother, I'll never forget my high school graduation! Thanks for the memory, my friend.

Bill Marlowe and Norm Nathan

Rock & Roll was born in the 50's and therefore is a part of my history. I bought my first 45 at a local drugstore on the corner of Park and Tenney streets, Morrissey's Drugs which later became Kluff's Drugs. It was Johnny Cash's *I Walk the Line*. On the flipside was *Get Rhythm*. I liked the flipside the best because I was shining shoes with my own personal shoe shine kit at the time on various corners and in the local barrooms. I was seriously interested in the art of shining shoes. And snapping my buffing rag rhythmically was important.

I sat through several showings of *Rock Around the Clock* staring Bill Healey and the Comets at the Star Theater but nevertheless I had a very short love affair with Rock & Roll. The girl in the movie who performed the exciting dances with the black hair and the pink underwear that became very visible each time she came sliding on the floor between her dancing partner's legs directly at the camera was another story.

I was at our rented cottage at Salisbury Beach for our family's annual summer vacation when I had an epiphany. My brother, Ernie, who was seven years older than me had started his first year of college at Northeastern University. Between his roommates and the Boston atmosphere he had become a jazz music buff. He talked endlessly about places like Storyville and Pall's Mall. No matter what station I

166

tuned the radio to, he kept changing it to some guy by the name of Bill Marlowe.

The first Jazz song I ever really listened to was *Draggin' My Red Wagon* by Anita O'Day. I still don't know what the red wagon refers to but it sounded super sexy and seductive when Anita sang it. And that classic was followed by *I'll build a Stairway to Paradise* – with a new step everyday by Sarah Vaughan. That was it! I was epiphanized or epiphanated or whatever. I have been hooked on Jazz ever since.

Bill Marlowe was not a Rock & Roll fan. He spoke very derogatorily of Rock & Roll. One of his infamous chants was, "Here on this show we play music. That's music spelled m-u-s-i-c and not n-o-i-s-e. He would introduce a song by saying, "Now folks let's listen to one by ELVIS PRESLEY ... (then there would be a long pause to put his regular audience in shock and finally he would add with a chuckle the possessive 's' sound and it would finish) Elvis Presley's good friend Erroll Garner or Al Martino, or Dakota Staton.

Bill Marlowe was born in the north end of Boston – in the Italian section. But when he started out in the 40's in radio nobody was hiring Italians. He had to change his name to make himself more appealing to the average listening audience.

One had to be persistent to keep up with Bill Marlowe. The radio stations dumped him every few months it seemed. He wouldn't play Rock. He would only play the music he loved – Jazz.

He began his radio career at WCCM – AM in Lawrence in the early 40's. I followed him from WBZ-AM to WILD-AM. It seemed like he was always moving and he would tell you where and why on the air. He wasn't going to prostitute himself and sell out to what was popular. It was Jazz or nothing. Bill was great. While all my buddies were listening to Woo-woo Ginsburg and Adventure Car Hop, I was tuned to WILD and the Bill Marlowe show.

In the 50's when the payola scandal broke out Bill would laugh on the air and say things like, "They ain't looking for me! They know no one is paying me to play Al Martino, Erroll Garner, and Dakota Staton." Bill died in 1996. He was the best.

Norm Nathan kept me up nights. He had a show on WHDH called Sounds in the Night. He loved Jazz and big bands. He played selections that never made it to daytime radio, like *Crescendo and Diminuendo in blue* – with an interval by Paul Gonzsalves – by the Duke Ellington Band at Newport in 1955. That one song took up nearly one whole side of the album. But what a song! After listening to that while lying in bed at midnight – you were up till 2 a.m. for sure. No sleeping after that.

Then Norm might play *Sing Sing Sing* by the Benny Goodman band at the 1938 Carnegie Hall concert with the famous Gene Krupa drum solo. That famous song was actually written by Louis Prima. You didn't hear sounds like that on Woo-woo Ginsburg.

He played a lot of Stan Kenton too. But on top of the great music the guy was a real clown. He did all these satirical skits and people would call in all night long. He would lead them on with bogus history about the guy who really discovered America rowing over from Europe in a paper mache' canoe and landing somewhere in Methuen. He was so authoritative and believable that people would say, "No kidding. I didn't know that." Norm Nathan was an original.

My interest in Jazz never dissipated. Not being able to sit still while listening to good Jazz, I bought myself a set of drums and joined in with all the greats in my parlor. I started playing the drums as a teenager – which was quite a torture for the neighbors and the other tenants at 32 Chelmsford St. Amazingly enough, I am just as good today on the drums as I was the day I started. It is really hard to believe – and at my age even more difficult. Very few people have ever heard me play the drums but those few that have, told me that is the way it should be. So that makes me feel good. Everyone needs to feel special sometimes.

At my ice cream parlor in Carrabelle I bought a karaoke and made my own imitation radio tapes. My ice cream parlor was called Hobo's and my radio station was WHOBO broadcasting from under the mile high tower in uptown/downtown Carrabelle at 98.6 on your dial. It was 98.6 because that's body temperature. My one requirement was that my listeners had to be alive. I was not into playing music or telling jokes to dead people.

I sang too. I called myself Vic the Moan. I didn't sing as well as I played the drums but eventually I developed a style of talking the lyrics like Jimmy Durante and Ted Lewis. I think I did very well – I never asked any of my customers. What the hell would they know? I figured it is MY ice cream parlor and if I was going to starve to death and go broke selling double scoops of ice cream at 1959 prices like I once got at Wasmaco's outside Canobe Lake Park, I could do it my way and with a song in my heart. My wife didn't complain either – but she has the unique ability to take her ears out at night and put them in a box on the bureau. She can spin a little doohickey and turn things off and on at her discretion during the daylight hours – one of the benefits of growing old. I, on the other hand, had to listen to myself. But I didn't mind. Over the years I have grown used to me. Hopefully you folks will have a similar metamorphosis one day also.

Phony Names

We periodically changed the location of our "Corner" by request of the local police department. But after a series of YEARS it got a little bothersome. And besides, we had used about every corner in our neighborhood at one time or another.

At first, when we were just little guys and the cops drove up in a cruiser, we ran. We all had our favorite hiding spots. I was always rather partial to a backyard garbage can.

The old garbage cans were 50 gallon drums. Most of them had lids on them. And there was sometimes a handle welded on to a lid. I would jump into a garbage can that was more or less empty, or only a quarter full. I would grab the lid by the handle and then pull it down on top of my chosen garbage can. The handle was now on the inside – with me.

If and when I heard someone prowling around the area outside my garbage can, I would lift my feet off the bottom and then hang from the handle. I don't remember what I weighed in those days, maybe 70 to 100 pounds, but it was enough to prevent any curious oppressor from peeking in on me. It always worked. I never got caught by anybody while hanging from a garbage can handle inside a 50 gallon drum, garbage can.

But as we grew older, things started changing. Along with puberty there were other rites of passage and running every time a cruiser pulled up to the Corner passed rather early on. We got to the point where we just sat there and stared back at the cops.

In the beginning the cops didn't really know how to act. They were accustomed to pulling up and having us all scatter. When we didn't they were somewhat confused as to what they should do. Was this action on our part an insult to their authority? Were we defying the system? Would we fight if they approached us? What was going on here?

Their first notion was that a more severe threat was necessary. The cruiser was no longer threatening enough for us little criminals. A further show of strength was needed. They would have to increase the pressure.

The cop would stare at us for a moment out the window of his cruiser – building tension. We would all stare back. He would then pick up his microphone or walky-talky and pretend to be doing something official. He would get out of his cruiser, jack up his trousers, adjust his gun belt, check his hand grenades and flamethrower and then swagger across the street – John Wayne style.

The first time a cop went through this ritual, I remember feeling a little antsy and asking myself why I wasn't running. But then as time passed and this experience grew in its repetition, the fear subsided. I imagine George "Machine gun" Kelly felt similar after his first engagement with the FBI.

"Okay," this cop on this particular occasion said, pulling a pad and pen from his shirt pocket. "You," he demanded pointing the butt end of his pen at one of us ten year olds. "What is your name?"

We had no idea what he was up to. We gave him our real names.

After he wrote down all of our names, he folded over his pad and clipped his pen back onto his pocket.

"Okay," he said. "I am going to be patrolling this area all day. I am going to come by this corner every so often. I have your names. So I know who each of you are. The next time I come back, if I find any of you guys on my list here again, you are going to be in for some real trouble. Now get moving and I would advise none of you to be back here again today."

We got up from our places and went meandering off for a walk around the block.

Well the fact that this flatfoot had to write down our names indicated to us that this particular cop didn't have much of a memory. We only had to see him once and we knew who he was. But he needed to take names.

We walked around the block and then returned to our designated squatting area. If he came back we all agreed we would just give him a phony name.

Sure enough an hour or two later our buddy with the bad memory was back. He pulled out his pad and pen once again. He looked us all over closely.

"Okay you," he said jabbing the butt of his pen in Jack Sheehy's direction. "What is your name?"

"My name is Petrobi Patsaiba."

"How do you spell that?" Jack spelled out something and the cop looked at him seriously for quite some time. Jack said nothing but stared him back in the eye.

He then pointed his pen at me and repeated his question.

"My name is Lance Guibe."

The cop put on a very nasty look. He knew by the strange silence and peculiar looks on our faces that something was up.

"Where do you live?"

"I live at home."

"Yeah, yeah ... I'm sure you do. Where the hell is your home, smart guy?"

"It's on the other side of town."

"What's the name of the street?"

"I don't remember."

"You don't remember the name of the street that you live on?"

"I don't have to remember. I know where it is."

The cop glared at me.

"You!" he said pointing to Jimmy Costello. "What is your name?"

"Francis DeSissy."

He then went to Russ Brown.

"What is your name," he asked Russ.

"My name is Richard Noble."

We all turned and looked at Russ in shock. What the hell was he doing? We had all agreed to give a phony name. Why was he giving the cop my name? Was he coo-coo or what?

"Noble, huh. I have your name here from the last time I was here. Where do you live, Noble?"

"I live at 32 Chelmsford St. It is just up a couple of blocks and to the left."

Russ, my good buddy, not only gave the cop my name but my address also – and then he went on to give directions to my house.

"Okay Richard Noble," the cop said returning his pad and pen to his shirt pocket once again. "You are in trouble. I will be contacting your mother and father and tell them what you have been doing. Now all of you scatter. And I don't want to see any of you back here again today."

We all slowly sauntered off as the cop returned to his vehicle and drove away.

"What the hell! Why did you give the cop my name, Russ? I thought we all agreed that we would give the cop a phony name?"

"I did give the cop a phony name. My name is Russ Brown."

"Yeah, I know your name is Russ Brown, but my name is Richard Noble, you butthead."

"I know that. I couldn't think up any good phony names like you guys did. All that I could think of was Richard Noble."

"Couldn't you have at least given him the wrong address?"

"I suppose, but all that I could think of was 32 Chelmsford St. It didn't seem right to say you lived on Spruce St. when I knew you lived on Chelmsford St."

"Well, that's real good, Russ. But I'm going to tell you something. The next time that cop comes back – if he ever does – you can be Richard Noble if it makes you happy but I'm going to be Russ Brown who lives on Arlington St."

"You wouldn't?"

"Oh yeah, watch me!"

"In that case," said Jack Sheehy. "I guess next time he comes I'll be Jimmy Costello. Jimmy, you can be Jack Sheehy. We'll really screw this guy up."

"Man, this is great! I love it," I said. "Nothing like hangin' out with a bunch of guys with a plan. Tell me Jack, what is the exact street address of your house? I wouldn't want to mess this plan up. It's a good one."

Bishop's Restaurant

Bishop's Restaurant was considered a landmark by anyone from my generation of Lawrencians. People came from all over and drove for miles to eat at Bishop's. Today that type restaurant is called a "destination restaurant."

I can remember sitting up on the wall at the Howard Playstead with a bunch of my buddies and having a fancy new model Caddy or Lincoln pull up and ask us for directions to Bishop's. We were always quite thrilled and proud to see fancy people coming to our humble tenement neighborhood to eat at one of our ethnic restaurants.

The original Bishop's was located in the Syrian district. I say Syrian. I know many were Lebanese and I'm sure there were some from other Arab nations as well. They were all Christians as far as I know. I don't remember any Mosques in the old neighborhood.

All the immigrants who came to Lawrence settled in a neighborhood where they felt comfortable. The houses were all similar throughout the city but one section would be mostly Italian, another Syrian, another Polish, and so on. The second generation would get more adventuresome and move here and there about the city. But the old sections would keep their ethic charm and solidarity, and good food.

The Syrian district spread around the Immaculate Conception Church. I don't recall all the street names that

175

comprised the district but let me guess at a few – Elm St., White St., Maple St., Chestnut St., Auburn St., and I think there was even a Lebanon St. Bishop's was in that area.

Bishop's didn't look like much from the outside but it was fancy on the inside. The booths were leather and the floors were carpeted. They had waiters rather than waitresses. This added an air of sophistication. I don't remember any other restaurant that had waiters. But then I was not a big restaurant aficionado in those days.

Lawrence was not a pretty neighborhood. I can imagine those Caddy and Lincoln people peeking out the door every five minutes to make sure their cars were still out there on the street. In my day a car might have been "borrowed" for a joy ride but never as part of a for-profit business enterprise.

The kitchen at Bishop's was filled with little, old, Syrian ladies. I know this because I delivered food stuffs to Bishop's new store in my truck driver days. The menu featured all sorts of Syrian specialties – stuffed grape leaves and stuffed squash were two popular items I remember. Hummus and Tahini was a unique dip I always ordered. The Hummus was made from chic peas and the Tahini from ground roasted sesame seeds. I heard the neighborhood Syrian women supplied the fresh grape leaves also. There was nothing like it.

I would get the Hummus and Tahini dip and a platter of stuffed grape leaves as an appetizer. I would squeeze fresh lemon wedges over the grape leaves then wrap the grape leaves in the fresh, still warm Syrian bread and dunk it into the Hummus dip. Oh yes! Was that ever good.

My main choice was always Lamb on a stick on a bed of rice pilaf. Bishop's was famous for its Shish Kabob but they also served steaks and Maine Lobsters and other conventional favorites.

And who could forget their heaping platter of homemade French fries. They had a giant potato peeler in the back at their new store, owned by brothers, Joey and Abe Bashara. The original store on White St. was started by mom who was known as "the Chief" and her three sons. Dad had died when the boys were young. Charlie, brother to Joey and Abe, died later on. The potato peeling machine had a big rough, round glob sized stone in its center. The stone spun around and scrapped all the skin off the potatoes. I never saw another one like it. The French fries were not straight and crispy. They were long, limp and potato tasting. I'll bet they were fried in lard too.

There was a Syrian bakery next to the old Bishop's that supplied their fresh Syrian flat bread. It was just around the corner. And the bread was made fresh daily.

Bishop's was a unique restaurant in a rather "difficult" neighborhood but their reputation swelled. And one day Joey and Abe Bashara built a palace of a restaurant right in the heart of town. It was at the far end of Hampshire St., a block or so up from Essex St. For Lawrence it was like the Taj Mahal. It had it all – cocktail lounge, huge, spacious, dining room, plush carpets, beautiful booths and tables. It was a wonderful, luxurious dining experience. For years it had a waiting line and reservations. I remember signing in and then going to the lounge. The lounge often had entertainment. This was all mighty fancy for old Lawrence but yet not expensive.

When I got word a few years back it had closed its doors, I couldn't believe it. It was certainly the end of an era for Lawrence. Who could imagine Lawrence without a Bishop's restaurant?

But Lawrence is without a lot of things these days. I suppose that is part of the reason for these columns. It seems such a shame to just let everything disappear. I suppose one day nobody will know such a thing as a Bishop's restaurant ever existed. The same goes for a Richard E. Noble also, I'm sorry to say.

My Mom and JFK

The phone rang in our little kitchen. We lived in a tiny apartment in Lawrence, Massachusetts. I spent the first twenty seven years of my life there. It was a mill town with layer after layer of blue collar tenement houses. My mother rarely answered the phone. It was usually never for her but someone calling for one of us kids. We all rushed to her side, ready to grab the phone when she said for whom the call was actually intended. But we were all stopped short, as she hung onto the receiver and began to speak; "Yes, I know who you are, Bobby. Yes, I know that it is your brother, John, who is running for president."

"What the ...? Who are you talking to Ma?"

"She's talking to Bobby; you know Johnny's brother." We all laughed, as she went on as if she were talking to one of our school chums.

"Yes, I realize that tomorrow is Election Day ... Oh yes, I certainly intend to vote for your brother. I understand ... Yes, I certainly will ... I will ... I will! I'm going to be there the first thing in the morning. I wish you and your brother the best of luck ... Oh, don't you worry Bobby. You have my vote."

Bobby Kennedy had called our house the night before his brother was elected President of the United States.

J.F.K was one of us!

An Irish Catholic, Massachusetts boy, was going for the presidency. This was as close to home as it could get – our little State, our maligned faith, our dumpy neighborhood, our blue collar apartment in the inner-city slum, and our telephone. It was unbelievable. My mother was talking to Bobby about the election; my mother who was probably the least political person I have ever known. But, that next morning she donned her winter coat and hat and went prancing off with her pocketbook hanging on her arm. I ran out on the porch. I didn't know whether to cheer, applaud or what. She looked like a miniature Eleanor Roosevelt parading down Chelmsford St. to the corner at Arlington where they were all lined up at the voting station.

She had received her orders and was marching to her destiny which was to personally elect John F. Kennedy president. And she did it. It was the closest election of the twentieth century thus far.

Johnny won by slightly more than 100,000 votes. He was the youngest man yet to be elected president – the first Catholic president. And though I was just slightly too young to vote for him myself, he was my president also.

He was the president of all the young people. He was as sharp as a tack. He knew his ABC's. He had all the answers. The press was no match for him. He was smarter than they were. He smiled, had a huge grin and told jokes about his dad and his wife and brothers and sisters. He was a big tease, just like an older brother, or your own dad. He was a hero during the war. I went to see the movie *PT-109* at the local movie theater. I bought his book, *Profiles in Courage*. I still have a copy. It was a real book.

Profiles in Courage was no political biography book about how I was born in a log cabin. It was not about himself. It was about men in history who had acted courageously, even if it meant sacrificing their political careers. John F. Kennedy was more than another pretty face.

Profiles in Courage was a book about ideals, about principles. It became a TV series. I can remember lying on the parlor floor with my head up against a hassock watching this week's excerpt with the whole family. At the end of each episode there was somebody crediting John F. Kennedy, and some bit of his personal idealistic inspiration. If I'm not mistaken, he introduced the show, or signed it off – or something.

John F. Kennedy, the war hero, who had saved his buddies; the intellectual and Harvard graduate, the journalist, the TV show writer, the first Catholic president, the youngest elected president, the family man with a picture book wife and regular kids hiding under his desk at the White House, the little rich boy who had a feeling for the working stiff. John F. Kennedy, the man who was going to bring peace to the world at last.

By the time I got to Merrimack College everybody was enrolling in the Kennedy Army for Peace. They called it the Peace Corps. They say that it was really Hubert Humphrey's idea, but it was Kennedy who pushed and promoted it. Every student I talked to was joining the Peace Corps. They were all making me feel guilty and hypocritical. Finally we had a president who stopped the tradition of talking about peace while making war; a president who was going to turn it all upside-down. He was going to actively make peace and try to keep the war mongers talking. The whole world got his message and everybody was cheering – except the Russians and Fidel Castro.

Then suddenly it was eyeball to eyeball. The end of the world was on the horizon. But this was O.K. It was all for one and one for all. It was no pull-a-name-out-of-a-hat deal. If we were going to die, we were all going to die at once – BOOM! And who gives a damn. It would be a relief. No more hiding under the desks, or looking for a designated bomb shelter, or storing up supplies in the cellar, or contemplating a slow death by some kind of horrid radiation poisoning. If the world really couldn't be saved, then let's end it, once and for all. We would prove T. S. Eliot wrong. The world wouldn't end with a whimper but a BANG! We finally got this chicken-chicken stuff over with. Khrushchev pushed, and Kennedy pushed back – the Cuban Missile Crisis.

When it was over Khrushchev had blinked. Russian ships were on the TV loading up their ships and heading home with their bombs and missiles. Kennedy had stood up to the bullies and they were tucking their missiles between their legs and heading back to their own schoolyard. If there was anybody who doubted Kennedy's policy at that time, I don't remember they had time to voice their opinion. The missiles were there; we were on the brink of destruction, and then it was over. It was scary, but we all went through it together – holding our breath.

I have heard many say Kennedy did it all wrong, we should have invaded Cuba and put Castro to rest. But information from the Russian Archives has since proved Mr. Kennedy and his brother were more than correct. The Russians had tactical nuclear weapons on Cuban soil and submarines off the East Coast of the U.S. with orders to fire if the U.S. had attacked. And due to problems in the Russian communications system the order to retaliate had been given by Khrushchev and couldn't have been changed in time to stay a holocaust. The East Coast of the United States from Washington D.C. to Tampa Florida would have been gone – along with a heck of a lot more. The incident scared the heck out of both Kennedy and Khrushchev and they consequently had the infamous hot lines installed.

But, Kennedy was a president to whom the presidency wasn't the culmination of his life and career. He was too young. He was just starting. He was going to be something special. He would write history or be a movie star, or teach at Harvard. The presidency was just a stop on his way to bigger and better things and everybody knew it.

I was in my college History class at Northern Essex Community College. It was a renovated Haverhill grammar school. It cost me one hundred and fifty bucks a semester. I had a 1946 DeSoto, fluid drive that had to be jump-started every day. I parked it on a hill outside the school and everybody watched and laughed each day as, my buddies and I, all pushed it down the hill to get it rolling and then jumped in when I popped it to a start. It was bright yellow, and we called it the Banana Boat. A phrase made popular a few years earlier by Harry Belafonte. This new junior college and the state-wide junior college program was one of Kennedy's new ideas. A kid of my social class, and my finances, and my academic background had very little hope of getting a college education before this program.

A young office worker stepped into our classroom, unannounced, walked up to the teacher's desk and handed him a piece of paper. The teacher read the note, silently. Then he looked up at the class, and spoke:

"The President of the United States has just been shot in Dallas, Texas. The class is dismissed."

A boy in the back of the class jumped up and started mumbling something about his tuition and that he was paying that teacher's salary and he wanted the class to continue. The teacher repeated; "Class dismissed." Then he turned and started gathering things up from his desk. The mouthy boy kept grumbling. He grumbled all the way down the corridor and out into the schoolyard. In a matter of seconds he had a crowd around him and was in a fist fight.

In the cellar of the grammar school we had a small make-shift cafeteria. It was just vending machines, a small bookstore and a couple of TVs. We were glued to the TVs. The girls were all in tears and sobbing. Their eyes were all wet and raw and their noses red from the constant use of tissues and table napkins.

My father had died suddenly and without warning a few years earlier. This assassination was the exact same experience all over again. Once again I was waiting for the doctors to announce that everything would be all right and he would live, but just as with my dad, this wasn't to be the case.

I was stunned in the same way as I had been with my dad when they announced that the president was dead. But, I was steeled to the concept of death now. I had no tears. I had no "whys." Death has no explanation. The Nation would go on as it did after Lincoln, after Garrison, after McKinley. It would go on as it has after all the different presidents who had been killed or who had died in office. We had a system, and the system would go on; just as my life had gone on after my father's death. Just as everyone's life continues and goes on after the death of any loved one. You have no choice.

But a lot of dreams would now die and be forgotten.

At my father's funeral, they kept saying he was so young. I thought, silently, does death have an age limit? Is anyone too young or not old enough to die? Hardly. Here was the hope of the world and he had just had his head blown apart in Dallas, Texas.

Watching the funeral on the TV was tragic. Little John-John being prodded forward by his mother and saluting the coffin; the horse with no rider; the hauntingly slow, and penetrating cadence of the drums – a whole nation in mourning. The memories of those days never seem to die.

Maybe they're not supposed to.

HAVE YOU READ THESE BOOKS BY RICHARD EDWARD NOBLE

Hobo-ing America
A Summer with Charlie
Honor Thy Father and Thy Mother
The Eastpointer
A Little Something
Noble Notes on Famous Folks
America on Strike
A Baker's Dozen

These books are available on the internet at the major vending sites.

Bookstores, libraries and other vendors can contact Noble Publishing at richardedwardnoble@fairpoint.net or Noble Publishing, box 643, Eastpoint, Fl 32328 for volume discounts.

HOBO-ING AMERICA

Seeing the U.S.A. clinging to the elbow of Carol and Dick will be an awakening for most Americans no matter how many times they have toured the U.S.A.

Come along with Carol and Dick and live in the places where Charles Kuralt was afraid to park his bus.

Feel the pain, joy and anger and shake the calloused hands that make America what it is.

See America in its glory and its shame. See it from the highways, the sidewalks and the gutters. Meet Asians, Indians, Jamaicans, Haitians, Mexicans. Meet most of them in one chicken factory in central Arkansas on the third shift.

See America from the bottom of the cracker barrel. Come along with Carol and Dick. Talk to the "Crackers" and fill the barrels.

HONOR THY FATHER AND THY MOTHER

Honor Thy Father and Thy Mother is a tragic novel. The main character is a little boy. The reader learns to understand Richard by listening to his thoughts. We read his mind as he tries to make sense of those around him. We follow Richard's thoughts from ages five to thirteen as he translates the people, the circumstances, and the society around him. The reader will walk through a tragedy of personal, religious and social confusion. Anyone who reads this book will be left with some very difficult impressions and many shocking images that will never go away.

The book is an attempt to distinguish between discipline and abuse, between a spanking and a beating, between being scolded and being harried, between learning and indoctrination. It is a journey through the rational and the irrational.

Honor Thy Father and Thy Mother is also a love story and it is a study in the nature of hate at the same time. It is about family and religion. It is about hard times and depression. It is about alcohol and alcoholism. It is about what is going on in the apartment upstairs or the tenement next door. It is real life – and death.

THE EASTPOINTER

My column *the Eastpointer* appeared each week in the Franklin Chronicle. In 2007 I won the first place award for humor from the Florida Press Association.

Eastpoint is in the Florida Panhandle, across the bridge from Apalachicola to the west and a few miles from the town of Carrabelle to the east. All three of these small communities are located in Franklin County on the Gulf Coast.

Franklin County has been, traditionally a seafood community. This volume contains a selection of columns that not only present the ideas and opinions of the author but create a portrait of life in the "sleepy, little fishing village" of Eastpoint. These stories are intended to be fun, entertaining and stimulate a laugh here and there. Hopefully they also contain a bit of wisdom along with the chuckles.

A LITTLE SOMETHING

A Little Something is a volume of poetry with prose. The volume is divided into several categories – My Hometown, Humor, Love and Other Nice Things, Tenderness and Tears, and On the Serious Side. The poetry is traditional in style and, as with all poetry, covers a wide range of interests and ideas.

BUT, DO YOU LOVE ME

But, do you love me?
And how would I know?
I look into your eyes, but the love doesn't show.
So how ... how would I know?
Days and nights, weeks and years,
Moments of laughter, and a lifetime of tears.

But do you love me?
And how would I know?
Nothing I see would tell me it's so.
We touch, we love, we laugh, we smile.
We cherish the moments, mile after mile.

But do you love me?
And how would I know?
Unless once in a while...
You'd tell me so.

NOBLE NOTES ON FAMOUS FOLKS

Noble Notes on Famous Folks was intended to be informative but yet entertaining – hopefully even humorous. I had great fun writing this book. I would like to do two or three more like it.

I was inspired to write a book in this style by stumbling onto a writer by the name of Willy Cuppy. Mr. Cuppy wrote a number of great books. His most famous is probably, *The Rise and Fall of Practically Everybody.*

My book states the basic facts of the people it describes with usually some not so well know tidbits thrown in. Many of the famous characters described in these pages are funny with no additional elaboration. There have been some really strange famous people – Abelard, Francis Bacon, and Tycho Brahe to point out just a few.

There are some who have stories that most people just wouldn't believe. For example: Archimedes, Alexander the Great, Walt Whitman, and even Charles Lindbergh. If you like history, you will love this book. If you don't like history because it is too dull and often written boringly, you will love this book. If you would like to read something and maybe learn a little something at the same time, this book is for you. Try it. I really think you will like it.

AMERICA ON STRIKE

If you don't know the
History of American Labor
you don't know
American History

I have come to the conclusion that the labor movement in America and around the world is the key to understanding or misunderstanding modern history. It is the Rosetta Stone to deciphering modern day politics.

The descendents of the Holocaust victims rewrite their story anew every generation vowing that it shall never be forgotten. It is the obligation of each generation to rewrite the past in the vocabulary of their times in order to keep it alive for all time.

This book is my small contribution to keeping the worker history of America alive for another generation.

A BAKER'S DOZEN

When I write about things that are common to my wife Carol and me, her comment is, "I love reading my husband's descriptions of our adventures. I get the enjoyment from the adventure I experienced and then the added pleasure of reading about the trip he went on." I guess I have been on a "trip" all my life.

All the stories in this book happened. They just may not have happened exactly as I have described them.

Big Jim was quite a man, a local hero to us kids. Cain and Bernard's barroom was the real thing. We all loved Walter, of Walter's Variety Store. Jeannie was the prettiest thing I had ever seen. Poor, little Howie, Gluckman with his gooey cigar, and Billy with his butcher's cleaver, I will never forget any of them.

Meet
Richard Edward Noble

Richard Edward Noble was raised in Lawrence, Massachusetts. He attended St. Rita's grammar school in Lawrence, Central Catholic high school also in Lawrence, Northern Essex Community College in Haverhill and Merrimack College in North Andover.

His mother and father and grandparents – on both sides of the family – were Lawrence textile workers.

Richard lived in Lawrence until the age of twenty-seven and then migrated to Fort Lauderdale, Florida where he met his wife Carol. Richard and Carol have been a team for over thirty-five years. They have both worked a variety of jobs. Richard has been a butcher, a dishwasher, an oysterman, a fruit picker, a restaurant manager and chef and the owner/operator of an ice cream parlor and sandwich shop in Carrabelle, Florida. These experiences and many more were published in *Hobo-ing America – A workingman's tour of the U.S.A.*

Richard is now retired and working as a writer. He writes fiction, non-fiction and poetry. He published a column in a local newspaper. In 2007 he received a first place award for humor from the Florida Press Association for this column.

Richard has a variety of interests – philosophy, history, politics, the American and world labor movements, economics, poetry, music, biography, autobiography and the unique history of Lawrence, Massachusetts.